HINTS IN HAIKU: *Japan's Pulse-beat*

HINTS IN HAIKU:
Japan's Pulse-beat

Norimoto Iino

PHILOSOPHICAL LIBRARY

NEW YORK

I had a Japanese dream
   Adorned with cherry blossoms
      In the guest-room of Southwestern.

Four lovely wood cuts
   Were hanging on the walls
      Of the college guest room.

Where does Japan begin
   Where does America end
      At this time of mutual love.

CONTENTS

Hints in Haiku

Chapter I   The Soul's Inmost Core: *Haiku*   15

Chapter II   Jen as a Way to Peace   68

Chapter III Zen as a Way to Peace   91

Chapter IV   Composed at Coe, BU, SUI   134

My Home

Sea-gulls cry
  White clouds glide
    Sail-boats dart

Swallows fly
  Huge ships glide
    Jet planes dart

White breakers defy
  Old habits slide
    Happy dreams dart

Big cities cry
  Fast trains glide
    New ideas dart

We loudly cry
  Peace must abide
    Bliss to all impart

My Class

Under a hawthorn tree
  White with flowery glee
    I offer a prayer for you

Under the hawthorn tree
  A year hence without me
    Think of my prayer for you

Without a hawthorn tree
  In all the years to be
    Think of God's trust in you

New Year

Japan takes on a charm
  As New Year hails her
    Under the gilded sky

Shiny icicles on the ground
  The pine-bamboo-plum ornament
    At each door will greet you

The children in colorful *kimono*
  Especially well-behaved
    Making polite bows to elders

The national anthem is being played
  Over the radio thus creating
    A thrilling atmosphere in the air

Japan destined to walk
  Ever on the highway of peace
    Is best symbolized by New Year

Poetic License

During the awful war years
   Many friends of mine were killed
      I died in imagination too

During those sad war years
   They mistreated me brutally
      I died in thought more than once

Now to this resurrected man
   Each sound is a song
      Each sight a shiny gem

Squirrels speak and solace
   Dews dance and dream
      To one who has thanksgiving

Time talks with triumph
   Space sparkles with splendor
      To one who has insight

God himself preaches
   A superb sermon on grace
      To one who is inspired

The hums, hues, aromas
   Of this uncommon cosmos
      All divine gifts radiant

A sojourner in a new place
   More susceptible to values
      Attributed to glorious God

Farewell to Coe

The time will soon come
    When I shall be saying
        Farewell to Coe College

My heart is filled
    With a million sentiments
        Joyous, grateful, overwhelming

One of my most delightful
    Years of all my life
        Has been this academic year

Through the purple succor
    Of eternal, Almighty God
        This has been a blissful year

You Coe colleagues and students
    Have meant a world to me
        As I was privileged to teach here

You Coe friends have taught
    This Japanese student old
        An infinite number of things

My grateful, heartfelt prayers
    Will be with you and Coe
        All the years to come

May He bestow upon you all
    Exactly the gifts you need
        As you carry on your noble task

The University of Cedar Rapids
    Is the way Coe will be called
        As she grows in stature years hence

Haiku Hints

Between my words and the world
  Hints in *Haiku* and history
    There is a one-to-many correspondence

Nobility, newly disclosed
  In the trivial routine
    One's own self and life itself

A new star swims into the sky
  Sublimity shines in the sordid
    Glory smiles in God's world

Separation would stand out
  To the casual eye
    Of petty provincialism

Unity and togetherness
  To the discerning eyes
    Of the highly disciplined

Twelve languages studied
  Quantum theory, mathematics
    International relations bespeak
            togetherness

The insight of the Bible
  The strange story of Zen
    Now verified in these four ways

My group philosophy
  Reveals the kaleidoscopic coherence
    Of all civilization

It is a rare interwovenness
  Of art, science, religion
    Throughout the history of mankind

Illness, humiliation, oppression
War, rigorous disciplines
Have taught me compassion

Disclosure of esoteric values
Nobility found in the commonplace
Appreciation of agony itself

So there is a one-to-infinity mapping
Between my words and the world
Hints in *Haiku* and history

Patience

History continues to teach
    Not the prowess of men
        But the patience of God

Anger, greed, pride
    Replaced by broad compassion
        Rooted in cosmic togetherness

Longsuffering is not a sign
    Of weakness but a symbol
        Of inner heroism and mastery

Tradition

Tradition continues to fascinate
    Only through self-transcendence
        In the direction of richer meaning

Haiku, like art, science
    Ethic, religion, philosophy
        Is a tradition of the Japanese

It continues to thrill us
    Only when it is constantly changed
        Into the symbol of a richer whole

Chapter I

The Soul's Inmost Core: *Haiku*

The shortest form of poetry we know is *haiku*. It is seventeen-syllabled. And yet it is moving, characterizing the Japanese mind with a singular aptness.

> *Haiku* contains
> The inmost core
> Of the human heart
>
> The soul is
> Poured into
> 17 syllables
>
> Though brief
> *Haiku* mirrors
> The whole world

There are eight famous scenic spots near the Lake of Biwa in the vicinity of Kyoto. On a cloudy day a *haiku* poet was asked to describe all of these places in one poem of 17 syllables. This request was responded to instantaneously by the composition of a *haiku* like this.

> Seven scenic spots
> Being behind the clouds
> I hear the bell of Mii Temple

The Japanese word *Mii* means invisible. Here his reference to Mii implies that the eight scenic spots are all hidden behind the clouds, which could not muffle the charming music of the temple bell at Mii. This punning on the two words, *mienu* (invisible) and Mii (name of temple), enabled this poet to include all these eight places in one *haiku*.

15

> *Haiku* conveys
> Sincerity from
> Heart to heart

> The deepest truth
> Is enshrined
> In one *haiku*

It is enjoyable to read and appreciate another's *haiku*. It is more enjoyable to compose *haiku* ourselves. It is a thrilling experience to satisfy the urge within us to express our thought in this form. This thrill is contagious. These days western teachers and pupils have come to love it. Hence the article which appeared in the Japan Times on 18 March, 1962, put at the end of this chapter.

Mrs. Cohen's appreciation of *haiku* is gratifying to us. It shows something of the fulfillment of our wish, namely mutual supplementation of East and West. This will result in a deeper understanding of the Indian sense of togetherness. The *haiku* composed by an American is richer in meaning than one composed by a Japanese, because the former has something new which the latter does not have. We are glad that the Japanese form of poetry, namely, *haiku*, is bringing about such a result of intercultural cooperation.

Haiku in Japan was made famous by a man named Basho, 1644-1695. It is in order for us to understand what he was and what he tried to accomplish. He was a son of a teacher of calligraphy. Already at the age of ten he began to study the art of composing *haiku*. And all the rest of his lifetime he continued to compose *haiku*, nurturing those who were interested in the same art. He wrote in order to call their attention to beauty hidden in obscurity.

> Chestnut blossoms
> At the eaves escape
> The casual eye

16

He who thinks deeply senses the pathos of life. Especially he who is on his way to a strange land is a case in point. Man is a traveller from birth to death, just as time, days months, years are "travellers" moving from eternity to eternity. Change entails readjustment on the part of a human traveller. Thus pathos is even more acutely felt. Basho composed the following *haiku* about pathos.

> The hut of grass
> Is now inhabited
> By a strange family

> Waves on the beach:
> Among small shells
> *Hagi* flowers are seen

> Move ye graves
> My weeping voice
> Is the wind of autumn

The pathos which Basho depicted was so moving that the reader of his *haiku* is inspired into being still for a while. Behind it is the weight of eternity or the accumulated meaning of history itself. All this is packed into seventeen syllables. No wonder it makes us speechless with thrill. We feel painful within us because of the impact of all this realization of the value of civilization. Then we are compelled to kneel before the Eternal to pray or to practice Zen on the soft grass of India.

Basho's view of Nature is akin to that of the Chinese poets of the T'ang Dynasty. They regarded it as friendly to them, sharing joys and sorrows with them, showing signs of sympathy and compassion for them. In short, Nature was the extension or penumbra of human friendship at its noblest. It cheers up the sad soul. Its hums and hues mean something which the soul needs at the particular moment when they are enjoyed. Basho once stood on the northern beach of Kisakata where he saw white *nebu* blossoms in the rain. It was evening and getting dark. He was tired. But the graceful appearance of those wet flowers was a revelation to him. They enabled him to transcend the barrier of space and time, making him visualize a Chinese beauty named Seishi with whom the King of *Etsu* presented the King of *Go*. Thus the charming sight and sound of Nature had for Basho a symbolic meaning of self-transcending buoyancy. He forgot himself for a while, travelling to a foreign land of antiquity where kings and queens danced and fought.

> The rainy Beach
> Dotted with *nebu* blossoms
> As enchanting as Seishi

Where Nature is charming the historically famous personages of China or India are visualized, gladdening the heart of the *haiku* poet. Thus Nature speaks, dances, complains, sings, prays with him.

Basho devoted all his life to *haiku*. He stands for three values. First, he composed *haiku* so as to deepen his own soul. This he achieved by becoming harmonious with Nature, thus drinking deep the beauty and meaning of the animate world. Here the assumption is the friendliness of Nature toward human beings and the initiative it takes so as to console them, provided they are willing to listen to its voice of helpfulness.

Second, he made trips that he might meet more friends and enjoy more lovely sights and sounds. This was due to his wish to perfect his own sense of appreciation of all unnoticed aesthetic values, hitherto unrecognized in Nature and human souls.

> How noble!
> The sun beam
> Coming through the foliage

This Basho composed when he observed on a northern trip that the sun beam was coming through the thick foliage which was above him. Even the darkest nook in society should have some graceful influence coming through walls of inhumanity. He aspired to be some such influence.

Third, he composed heartfelt *haiku* in order to make others rejoice and profit society in general. This is what he has done for posterity. We today read his *haiku* and take heart again. He would call our attention to nobility found in the commonplace scene and happening. *Haiku* is not didactic but *subtle, suggestive, serene.*

> The Spring eve:
> Even the temple bell
> Is unheard

He who is preachy is not listened to. The truly loving glance is one that covers up and veils. Der wahrhaft liebende Blick ist zudeckend, verhüllend.

> Spring is departing
> Birds make music
> Fish have tearful eyes

Human voice is often too harsh. Nature, with the moon and the cloud, is quiet, but sometimes eloquent and moving. Basho aspired to emulate this unassuming music of Nature. Hence his *haiku*-composing.

Haiku is a miniature philosophy. It compresses the meaning of life into three short lines of poetry, thus depicting it with a vivid brevity. It has a few traits which may be briefly summarized as *enchanting, ennobling, eternal.* Basho's *haiku* would illustrate this.

> Enchanting and ecstatic
> But gradually pathos creeps in
> My cormorant-fishing boat

> Such noble fragrance!
> Of what flower it is
> I do not know

We could think of another set of three meaningful words *pensiveness, profundity, penetration,* which might reveal another dimension of this tradition. In view of life's transitoriness we become pensive. But this is an occasion for seeing more profoundly, thus penetrating in thought more deeply into life's wonder. Basho once realized that the garden of the temple which he was enjoying in late autumn was one hundred years old. The passage of one hundred years had added something to the moss-covered yard of that temple.

> The maple leaves falling
> Match the dignity of
> This time-honored temple

Again *haiku* is *calm, compassionate, contagious.* It is not noisy, does not advertise, does not broadcast. But it somehow lets us respond to its grace.

> The orchid fragrance
> Seeping into the wings
> Of a fluttering butterfly

Gratitude, grandeur, glory are three earmarks of this Japanese art. On the surface life is gray, full of ingratitude, and sorrowful. *Haiku* sees through the gray fog of life's surface into hidden grandeur, thus bringing the feeling of gratitude for the multi-dimensional glory of life's meaning and mystery. Basho implies all that by writing this *haiku*:

> Sublimity! They honor
> The straw coat and hat
> Even when it does not snow

The raincoat and rain hat are not useful on a bright, sunshiny day. But Basho, being a traveller, remembers the ways those helped him when it snowed heavily in the past. They will always shield and protect him in the future, when it snows. This retrospect and future promise add glory to the straw coat and straw hat hanging on the wall on a fine day. Their past utility and future helpfulness adorn the hat and coat with a halo.

Once Basho stood near a temple called Myoshoji Temple, situated near a pond. It was late autumn and the maple leaves were falling. He was much moved by the impressive scene, even more by boundless compassion which the temple symbolized. Somehow tears of gratitude began to run down his cheeks:

> Dyed by my tears
> Of gratitude
> The maple leaves fall

> Dawn is breaking:
> Still I long to envisage God
> Among the cherry blossoms

Haiku has another trait, described by three more adjectives, *humble, humane, holy.*

> The rice plant bows
> More and more lowly
> As it grows ripe

> All men are
> Brothers in
> All the world

> Smiles are
> The *Kimono*
> Hiding sacrifice

The meaning of *Haiku* is still more deeply disclosed through the use of another three words: *solitariness, surprise, sanctity.*

> Acutely do I miss
> My deceased parents
> When the pheasant sings

21

The lotus flower
Proves to be a Buddha
To discerning eyes

The cloud peaks
Are clearly pictured
At the bottom of the lake

Poise, pleasure and *power* are able to characterize *haiku* still further.

The soul which blesses
All men is able to
Enjoy heavenly peace

To do creative writing
Will bring pleasure
Unspeakable and great

Haiku-composing
Fills me with
Power, pure and clean

Haiku has three other ideals to represent. They are *sympathy, sincerity, subdual.* Our self-expression is lovely when it is sympathetic and sincere. But the Japanese taste is such that this spontaneous sincerity is controlled by humility, sympathy and thoughtfulness.

Issa, 1762-1827, represented this combination of spontaneity and subdual. Even when he was overjoyed he said something subdued.

This New Year
My happiness
Is rather medium

His *haiku* makes us smile, respond, thus influencing us deeply.

22

Haiku by Issa
Does teach me
To be kind

Issa stands for realism. His vivid imagination is felt in these *haiku*:

Suffering down on earth:
So the moon is eclipsed
Due to vicarious sorrow

Ah, full moon, autumnal,
I've been a co-traveller of yours
These fifty-seven years

The thin crescent
Looks curved:
How cold!

There are thistles. And so
Some worms prefer
Them to softer grass

Morning after morning
The nightingale
Has a rehearsal

Haiku is *unique, universal, useful*. Its uniqueness is a universal appeal. The mind may be tired of logic, cold and rigorous. Then *haiku* is a refreshing change to the tired mind.

Come to me
And play with me
Ye motherless sparrow

Issa lost his mother when he was three years old. Society was unkind to him. He was disinherited. Hence his wish to console a sparrow without a parent.

Science may advance further, life remains the same in its

solitariness, frustration, misuse of power. *Haiku* attempts to see unexpected consolation in the midst of the inhumanity of man and the vicissitude of history.

Philosophy in Japan is becoming more and more scientific and mathematical. Findings of social science and natural science continue to enrich it. But what is unique about it is its usage of intuitive, imaginative forms of expression like *haiku* and *waka,* in order to express the typically Japanese sentiment of appreciation and gratitude. Here *haiku* fulfills the task of adding a unique flavor to the scientific framework. It is *imaginative, interconnected, infinite.* Just as the sunset paints the whole western sky with crimson, vermilion, purple, so *haiku* adds an artistic appeal to the whole philosophy of science.

> Very similar
> To each other;
> *Haiku* and i

Galois once gave a legitimate membership to the imaginary number i in the mathematical cosmos, thus illumining all the dark nooks and corners of this cosmos with new meanings. The imaginary number is thus fulfilling a Christlike task of mediating between areas, hitherto labelled discrete. Mathematicians see infinity behind the simplest number such as 3 or 5. So *haiku* bespeaks the infinite richness of life. A tiny violet which charms you as you are coming over the long mountain range, or the butterfly which looks sound asleep, perched on a huge temple bell, is a symbol of the infinite richness of our life itself, as it is safely sustained by the boundless compassion of ultimate reality.

> Coming over the hills
> I am strangely charmed
> By this violet

> Perched on
> The huge bell
> The butterfly sleeps

Artistry

Artless artistry
  Is the sole virtue
    Of *haiku* poetry
Mugiko no giko ga torie *haiku* kana.

Suggestiveness

Haiku means
  The suggestiveness of a dream
    The peak of a rainbow
Haikudo yoin jojo niji no mine.

Jewels

Though small
  Yamato songs
    Are jewels
Chisaku tomo kagayaku takara yamato uta.

Artless

Be true to yourself
  As you wish to be
    As you wish to say

No distortion
  No exaggeration
    No compulsion

Like the stream
  Flowing down
    Merrily and with music

Your noblest self
  Is expressed simply
    With artless artistry

A genius is
Akin to a child
Who sings in a dream

Beyond Boredom

The flower of *haiku*
No boredom brings
Enchantment endures
Kentai wo umanu yamato no uta no hana.

Beautiful God

Illumined by the greenness
Of early Summer breezy
The grace of God embraces all.

Kaze kaoru shoka no midori ni teri haete
yorozu ni so so gu kami no mimegumi

Subdued

The Japanese soul subdued
May be understood
By western students bright

Deep Thought

Deep thought
Lies curled
In *haiku* and *waka*

Ah, Truth

Ah, Truth!
  Thou art all
    The soul of God

Dr. Hayao

Spring has come round,
  Trees are green; the sun shines
    His kindness is like all that

Children

Children are all
  Rare philosophers
    Who wonder and doubt

Yamato Co-existence
(Yamato means Benign peace)

Shinto, Buddhism and
  Confucianism mutually enrich
    In the land of *Yamato*

Togetherness

The togetherness
  Of all things is
    The source of value

A Strange Charm

A strange charm fills me
As I take my pen
To compose *haiku*

Pain Perishes

Haiku steals away unaware
All forms of suffering
To which the soul is heir

Haiku akin to Romance

The way of romance
Is somehow akin
To the charm of *haiku*

Muni
(Quiet Sage)

Seventeen syllables:
A hint that we should be
Ever sparing in words

A Mirror

Haiku is a mirror
In which we see
Noble quietness

Poetic Joy

Poetic ecstasy
    Is the stuff of which
        Haiku is made

Long Thought

Though short,
    Long thought,
        Deep meaning

No Wickedness

The brevity of *haiku*
    Is no symbol of
        Wicked taciturnity

Togetherness

Philosophy sees
    All things of the world
        In their togetherness

Lovelier

Carefully inspected,
    Life and the earth
        Are lovelier than dreams

Sincerity

The heart of *haiku*
  Is magnanimous
  And gracious

Benign Peace

Beauty and bliss;
  This is the soul
    Of *Yamato* Peace

Westernization

Westernization
  Must be done
    With thoughtfulness

Teachers

America and Russia
  Are good teachers
    For me, a learner

China and India
  Are wise teachers
    For a student like me

Pleasure

Haiku-composing
  The most innocent
    And exalted pleasure

India

Weeping under the cruel fate
  Of the blade and blood . . .
    Lo, a noble dream in the mental sky

Prayerfully

In this place of learning
  Prayerfully do we foster
    This friendship of ours

Radhakrishnan

Plato's dream
  Has come true
    In India today

United East
  And West
    Radhakrishnan

Bring about peace
  From Asia
    Oh, philosopher

Vedas

Various flames
  But behind them
    Is one fire

Art

A blue bridge
    Spanning past and present
        Is art, undying

It combines
    Past fragrance
        And future dream

Where on earth is
    The kind thoughtfulness
        Of the benign soul?

The sound of wooden clogs;
    The pyramid in the moonlight:
        Ah, unique impressiveness!

Peony Snow-flakes

Fluffy snow-flakes
    Wafting down softly
        Even more softly

Large snow-flakes
    Coming down slowly
        Over the flower garden

Spring snow-flakes
    Wafting down softly;
        Whose house are ye visiting?

Parachutes
    Or jelly fish?
        No. Peony snow flakes

God in You

You are bright
  In the sight of God
    Who sees promises

You are strong
  For He is with you
    Through Christ Jesus

You are bliss
  For He blesses
    Your souls pure

The Cross

Out of pain
  Come sterner virtues
    Like longsuffering

God works
  Through disvalues
    Like humiliation

Resilience
  Arises from
    Agonizing sorrow

He transforms
  All suffering
    Into blessing

Death itself
  Is unable to
    Stop our pilgrimage

Our immortal
   Journey guided
      By eternal God

Marks the shining
   Courses throughout
      God's eternity

Dr. Maurice E. Troyer's Mother
(Feb. 13, 1964 was her 89th birthday)

Your longevity
   A shining symbol
      Of God's approval

My prayer:
   May you ever be
      Abundantly blessed

How noble!
   That soul of yours
      Devoted to God

Your life is
   A living witness
      To the love of Christ

Heaven and earth
   Are truly full of
      The grace of God

   Maurice Troyer's Mother

A good wife and wise mother
   Serving God, having helped a pastor
      The spring of the eighty-eighth year
      Enjoying life eternal right here

My Mother

The memory of her childhood days
Is that of peace, plenty, merrymakings.
She, a rich farmer's daughter
Beloved by kind, country folk.
But love of truth made her discontented
With the sunny farm and the golden harvest.
Thus began her schooling in a large city
With missionaries to teach her
And the charm of the faith of Christ.
But the irony of fate led her
To marry a Shintoist statesman.
Then followed her days of suffering and tears,
Bitter disagreement prevailing in the home.
And yet what has made her live
Is her love of literature, history
Her trust in the promises of a son.

Free Thinker

The valedictorian
Speaks with poise
On freedom of thought.

This young person
That day commences
A new era of hope.

Men must not be
Ostriches with their
Heads stuck in the ground.

We look up and
See our maker, who is
The source of all truth.

Our glances, upward,
Hopeful, adventurous
And creative originality.

The Golden Cross
Of Christ towers
Up to the zenith.

No end set to
The soaring imagination,
The mother of invention.

In midheaven
There is no barrier,
No rigid regimentation.

The eternal sky
Steeped in the sunbeam
Of all-loving God.

Infinity and eternity,
The earmarks of
Our life, learning, love.

Dawn, morning, noon,
Afternoon, twilight, sunset
The million stars.

The rhythm of the
Galaxies, great and glorious
Marks the greatness of our God.

The choir of the cosmos is
Our valedictorian
Bespeaking God's peace.

This peace is the source
Of our prayer and hope
Which recur through all ages.

In a small office
Teacher and pupil,
Dawn of a new age.

Three girls and a teacher
In a sunny room
Ah, the hope of this world.

Mt. Fuji over the horizon
Smiles with us
As beauty, truth are discussed.

The Musashi Field
Purple with felicity
Surrounds us.

A happy class
Where tea is served
Understanding prevails.

Spring

Ah, the reddening
Of the crimson plum tree:
There a hope infinite curls.

Kobai no
Edani mugen no
Nozomi ari.

Red and green
Adorn the top
Of the peach tree.

Young leaves:
A happy contrast
To the color pink.

Mutually enriching
And stimulating:
Teacher and pupils.

The Foliage Speak

The Spring Rain
Quietly and with grace
Reviving the earth.

The foliage deliver
A speech on beauty
With a benign tone.

Life's roughness
Is transcended
When the rain sings.

Joyous Spring

Spring has come
My child is in ICU
I have chance to think

Haru Kitari
Chojo nyugaku
Ware shisako

April 5, 1962

The sky is blue,
Willow trees are green,
Peach blossoms redden.
The weather is noble
On the morning of April 5.

Sora asagi yanagi midori ni
Momo akaku shigatsu itsukano
Asano kaisei.

April 20

Young leaves, yellow and red
Mark this garden of study
Here in the Musashi Field.

Kini akani mo yuru wakaba no
Musashino ni kokoro tokimeku
Manabi yano sachi.

The hedge of friendship
Dear and divine
Adorned with bright foliage.

Natsukashimi mata itsukushimu
To mo gaki wo kazaru shigatsu no
Wakaba kagayaku.

All young leaves
Look heavenly,
Even Fatsia Japonica.

Yatsude sae subete wakame wa miyabiyaka.

Religion

Religion does not flourish
Because of its narrowness
And exclusive-mindedness.

Christ came
To bear witness
To God's truth.

Ah, Order!
Thou art all
The soul of God.

Philosophy, Art
And Science too
Serve God in Christ.

Self-forgetting is
The first step
Toward enlightenment.

Enlightenment
Is to understand the self
By forgetting it.

Compassion makes
A friend
Out of the enemy.

Soft-heartedness
Will win the foe
In the long run.

Ah, the breadth
To learn from
All the world history.

You are witnesses
Of the noble prayer
Of Christ, the Lord.

We are here
To be framers
Of a new history.

Only one sheet
Of paper is enough
For the Gospel.

Let us stress
Not only sin but
The deed of love.

We should pray
That His will
May be done.

Ah, the soul
Spacious
And humble.

Ah, this campus
Of shining faces
And the green foliage.

Yamato means
The land of benign peace
Which is enduring.

Time

Time cures, consoles:
It also beautifies
In this life of ours.

Sometimes life is
Too much with
Us susceptible souls.

Time is invisible,
Intangible also
But it works ever.

God is in time,
Thus healing
Our inner wounds.

41

It sweetens
Our past, thus breeding
Hope, joy and strength.

Enlightenment

Not word but soul
Is the key to
Enlightenment.

Dogen, 1200-53

The vale voice and mount hue are all mercy.
The self transformed becomes enlightened.
The temple bell ever bespeaks compassion
Rooted in One Crimson Heart of Cosmic Love.

The Class

Three members
Of this class.
Kennedy, Khruschchev, Castro.

God conducts it
With love, grace,
Convincingness, too.

Kennedy asks
Good questions
Thus learning much.

Khruschchev disagrees
But is ultimately
Convinced by God.

Castro is excited
But is quieted down
By His calm patience.

42

The rest of the world
Is an auditor
Treated kindly too.

This is the ideal
Of global education
Which God conducts.

Duty in Beauty

Beauty beckons to all
Those who are appreciative
Of the mystery of life.

Spring clothes the world
With the unspeakable
Charm of fresh green.

Its aroma and fragrance
Are irresistibly sweet
To all who love beauty.

Each day sees the deepening
Of the shades of leaves,
Flowers and blossoms.

Why is beauty beautiful?
The Thoughtful ask?
Here is the answer from above.

Beauty is indeed a puzzle
Until it is seen
In relation to love divine

Beauty is a duty,
Another occasion on which
We should be thankful.

Thankful for this charm
So universally present
In the world divine.

Beauty purifies, ennobles,
Transforms our beings,
To be devoted to the Highest.

Loveliness is His Love
For all those who live
And have their being in Him.

A joyous occasion of praise
Is beauty, whereas frustration,
A poignant occasion of worship.

Beauty is a gift great
From God who is
The Giver of all good gifts.

Out of gratitude to His Love
We devote ourselves to Him:
This is our joyous duty.

The Cosmic Sponsor of Value,
The Axiogenesis, Axiosoteria,
The Fellow-sufferer who understands.

The Great Companion is
The Cosmic Concreter
Urging Coordination everywhere.

The Loveliest

The loveliest of all men
Are the lowliest children
Who are humble and pure

Men of possessions
And prestige are away
From God and His grace

Not in the privileged seat
Of the proud and secure
Is God and His love

In humility and poverty
Can we find nobility
Such as what God approves

The lowliest are the loveliest
The solitary are the noblest
Christ was alone on the cross

How to Compose Haiku

Express spontaneously
What's felt sincerely
The form comes of itself

Three lines shiny
Mean three facets
Of the inner life

Use simple words
Depict vividly
Making the end strong

A unique style
Befitting yourself
Will soon be found

The joy of creation
Is what you'll enjoy
In composing *haiku*

45

The form is old
But it can embody
A new content unique

There is more freedom
In *haiku* of ours
Than in a sonnet

Beauty is joy,
Hope, bliss, thrill,
The source of poetry

The shortest form
Of poetry is *haiku*:
Three drops of ecstasy

Ecstasy is ours
As we write it
Sharing it with friends

Let it truly be
A harbinger of
The gladness of the world

Internationalists

Our vision goes beyond
False barriers national,
Racial, traditional

We pray for a world
Of freedom, justice,
Peace, shining, lasting

The vulgar world,
Narrow, dogmatic
Cannot see our truth

46

Only in this nuclear age
Does Christ's vision reveal
Its eternal validity

Who are international?
Christ and Confucius,
Buddha and Bunche

We students and faculty
Of this new school, ICU,
Which makes history bright

Learning from the past
And yet pioneering
Into a new elevation

God is ever
The uniquely good
Teacher of ours

All the happening
On which our eyes fall
Is the Dharma

Praying ever
And ever more
We go through life

The room is cold
Unheated, but
Our faith shines ardently

The voice of
The friends who prayed
With me is dear

God is a mirror
Disclosing the inherent greatness
Of each creature

47

Donna and Judie

Ah, the joy of meeting
The distinguished parents of
Two bright students of mine

My prayer is always:
May Donna and Judie,
Their parents be blessed

May God guide us
To realize a better understanding
Between the nations

The Sabbath sunbeam
Of Tokyo bespeaks
The profound grace of God

Christ is leading
Us to become
Peace-makers, effective and gracious

Kindness Here

The bus bounces
Like a wild horse:
Passengers groan

It is a veritable
Hell we must be
Suffering twice a day

But one can be
A Christ to his
Fellow-sufferers there

A little kindness
In word and deed
May brighten the bus

A great renovation, yes,
But until then, something
Can be done here too

The world is a bus
Where people groan,
Suffer, complain, die

A great renovation, yes:
But until then, something
Can be done there too

No cross, no Christ
No suffering, no solace,
No trial, no truth

God works in gall
No sin, no salvation,
No humiliation, no hope

All men must be
One in spirit, love
That encircles the earth

Spring is lovely
Its February intimations
Are fascinating too

Peace is great
Our prayers for it
Are thrilling too

Scholars are good
Young students too
Have equally great charms

Not consummation alone
But striving and stress
Are equally meaningful

Let us bless God
For each loveliness
In each stage of life

Too much pessimism
In this great age of ours
Let us stand for hope

Open minds and free
Usher in optimism
Which illumines darkness

God omnipotent
At work even in
The obscurest nook:

The orchid blooms
Under the foliage
Of thorns and thistles

Its fragrance fills
The entire valley
To please God alone

The serene power
Of the wintry noon:
How divine, invigorating

I love a crowd
Of all kinds of people
Who teach and thrill me

They are different
From one another;
Hence their value to me

Their background,
Their cultures, views, stands,
Their hopes, fears, prayers

All this is truly
Enlightening to me
As I deal with them

Once in a while
I am all by myself
And enjoy my privacy

The most precious
Of all eternity
Is the present moment

Good is done
Only in this
Divine moment

What we do now
Adds meaning to
The past and future

Eternity itself
Has any importance
Through work well done now

God is in
This present moment
Which shines with gold

Already in February
The willow twigs
Become full of life

They swing to and fro
In the breeze
As the sunbeam gleams

How graceful and noble
Are the bud-adorned
Willow twigs which shine

51

Soon they will put out
Green, yellow leaves
Like a cascade of spring

The willow is patient,
Swinging to and fro,
Never breaking, but enduring ever

Philosophy

Learning from the past,
Its values, insights and mistakes,
The thinker assembles his data

The East teaches patience,
Quiet persistence, mercy,
Resilience and peace-making

The West teaches analysis,
Experiment, mathematical thought,
Adventure, zest and hope

Christ mediates between
God and mankind, East and West,
The datum self and the ideal self

Between history and peace,
The world and the Kingdom,
Matter and the spirit

The Christ-inspired soul
Stands reempowered
To transform and create

Two Faces

Within the soul weeps
Under the weight of care,
Beaten and bruised

He weeps within
But smiles buoyantly
That he may comfort

He who is to see God
Must suffer more
Than all others

Weeping inwardly
But smiling outwardly
He did his tragic best

Writing, creating,
Helping all those
Who came near him

Dying of consumption
He planted the seeds
Of hope amidst despair

Christ continues to
Work in Kierkegaard
Weeping, writing, dying

Not Apathy but Appreciation

Life is gray, dry and sad
Study is boredom and frustration
The soul is dead and in despair

There is too much restriction
The noble spark of the spirit
Is forgotten by teacher and pupil

We need inspiration such
That shining possibilities of good
May be seen within each soul

Appreciation arises by comparing us
With those who are unable
To receive a higher education

With those who look back upon
Their college days long gone by
With those who died in war

Each problem has in it a gem
With its rare lustre and privilege
To those who are appreciative enough

Appreciation is the greatest thing
Missing in this world of haste,
Hatred, hurry and hollowness

Concentration is possible
Where there is a decision
To master a task excellent

Take up the cross of hardship
Willynilly found in achievement
In our academic, social fields

This is the rare meaning of
Christian discipleship in college
Where problems are privileges

Cooperation is possible
Where there is recognition
Of hidden guidance from above

God is the ultimate guide
In all enterprises, sublime
In and outside of our class-room

As I write these lines
The Musashi field gleams
Over my mental horizon

My students from overseas,
From Germany, India, China,
The Philippines, Korea, Hawaii

These bright folk truly are
Makers of a new history
Adorned with joy, bliss, peace

The rhythm of appreciation
Is the emblem of our ditty
Which is sung with gratitude

Gratitude to the Highest
Is the culmination of
Our song, sincere and serene

His banner over us is love
Which is like a huge blossom
White, cosmic, infinite, eternal

Let us pray ardently and always
That our whole beings may be
Refilled with its fragrance divine

There is nothing common on earth
In this temple of God's grace
Marked with a trillion chrysanthemums

Flower-filled, fully fragrant
Is this cosmos created
By our Benign God in Christ

Peace

Peace worthy of the name
Is joyous cooperation
And mutual enrichment

From any deterrent
Let us be all free
Let God be the guide

Nuclear Deterrents

We have no real peace
In this world of cold war
When nuclear deterrents keep peace

Too many folk are torn within
Frustrated, neurotic, afraid
Panic-stricken and ashamed

Prejudice is marked everywhere
Distrust, hatred, revenge
Swirl in too many hearts

Peace comes only when
Christian love purges inner lives
Laws, groups and nations

The world must be born again
Through the grace of God
Who works in eternal Christ

Miss White

Miss White in a Tokyo home
Sharing an eight-mat room
With her Japanese sister

Who studies all the time
Taking naps from time to time
With her head on the desk

Miss White is culture-shocked
Because her sister is evasive
Setting the alarm clock at dawn

Japan is a land of enigmas
Which puzzle the new comer
As she observes, listens, thinks

The biggest city of the world
Is crowded, noisy, rainy
With train collisions, double, triple

People here are tender-hearted
Soft-spoken and quiet
Only babies are extra noisy

Miss White is homesick
For straightforward folk
Humorous, optimistic, gay

Frame a History

Crowned with Mt. Fuji
The autumnal woods gleam:
Here we study, sing, pray
For benign peace to come

Christ, our Lord, divine;
The Sole, Supreme Symbol
Of God, Cosmic Composer
Of songs, noble and rare

Let us sing the song
Of hope and blessedness:
We of this great school,
Framing a history, shining bright

. . . .
With those who have come from overseas
To join us, we pray and talk together
. . . .

57

The world at its best is now here
Because you people have come
Unique joy and inspiration
Gratitude for the sea of God's concern

Change through Christ

To follow Christ
Means to comprehend
And transmute culture

Listen to tradition
Which speaks at least
Seven languages

Beauty, peace, muni,
Tao, Jen, quantum,
Mathematical expansion

Be more excellent   Mt. 5:20
Than all these:
Christ whispers ever

Change through Christ
Culture elevated into
Purer, diviner levels

The sinner speaks: II Cor.3:18
Changed from one degree
Of glory to another

Christ views sinful Japan   Lk. 5:10
In terms of possibilities
Of future fruition

He came not to abolish
But to fulfill all
This seven-faceted tradition

58

God in Christ is
The unique transmuter
Of disvalues diverse

Especially solitariness,
Estrangement and
Humiliation poignant

Beauty is liberated
From sentimentalism
Amoral and atheistic

Peace made more lasting
Than just characteristic
Of this post-war era

Muni, Tao, Jen are
Interested in the same task
Of bringing about peace

We Christians should be
More excellent than
All these peace-makers

Science seen in relation to
Service to God in Christ
And his peace enduring

New insights into *mathema*
Are self-disclosures
Of God eternal

Exclusive-mindedness
Would shut itself out
From the world of God

Not to criticize but
To comprehend and
Convert is our task

Christ views all things
In terms of possibilities
Of future fulfillment

Potentially ICU is
The forerunner of
The Kingdom of God in Christ

How big and benign
Are our souls? This
Determines our destiny

Conversion comes only
Through comprehension, change
And sublimation superior

Irony

Quantum theory shows
One indivisible universe
Including all its observers

Here is realized
The unity for which
Ethic has always hoped

It is ironical that
This world of quanta
Engenders the greatest peril

The cosmos of mathematics
Also is more unified
Than the world of men

But this cosmos is
So esoteric that it eludes
The view of common sense

God in Christ reigns
In all these three worlds
Of quanta, *mathema,* men

Peace will come when
These three are seen
In relation to God in Christ

War Cause

"Enemy soldiers are
Here to kill your
Loved ones at home."

This is the way
War begins each time
When nations fight

"War to end all war
To make the world
Safe for democracy."

"Make all Asia come
Under the shelter
Of one benign union."

These are slogans
To spur innocent
Folk to stand with arms

The enemy soldiers
Will never come here
If you are peace-makers

Foreigners are not
Brutal. They too pray,
Aspire, and long for peace

War never begins
Unless exceptional
Atrocities are advertised

War slogans are all
Such atrocities seen
In the so-called enemy

Big people kindle
The fire of brutal war
To kill idealistic young men

This should never be
Repeated in this world
Where the God of love reigns

He says: "Do not revenge."
Forgiveness unconditional
Is the only way out

Love endures all things;
Hopes, prays, plans
All things constructive

Cooperation comprehensive,
Contrition constrained,
Christ-consoled conviction

The Japan Times, March 18, 1962

Readers in Council

———

Haiku by U.S. Junior High School Students

To the Editor:

On Sunday, March 4, 1962, the New York Times printed
an article on page 31 written by A. M. Rosenthal. In this
article, Mr. Rosenthal reported that students at the Green
Farms School, in Westport, Connecticut, had written *haikus*.
This article was of particular interest to us.

The eighth grade students of Huntington Junior High School in Jamaica, New York, have also been writing *haiku*. The *haiku* has a boundless fascination and charm for our young people. This form of writing offers an opportunity for sounding emotional depths, stimulating the imagination, exploring values, and enriching experiences.

The *haiku* also offers an avenue to creative living. The eyes, ears, and hearts of our young people are awakened. As a result experiences are enriched. Enriched experiences offer further material for *haiku,* and so the cycle begins again.

The initial step in writing a *haiku* is taken when students are asked to tell their spontaneous associations to a given word. Spontaneity in response is encouraged. The response of one student stimulates the response of 10 students. The direction of the responses may be in range or in depth. For example the word "rain" brings forth such responses as: fishing, patter, puddles, spring, clouds, white caps, rainbow. Instead of continuing on in range the exploration of one response to rain may be pursued in depth. For example, the word "rain" brought forth these associations: stormy night, wet, cold, haunted houses.

Students are then asked to make a selection from the various thoughts or feelings recorded and to combine them into three short lines of writing. Unnecessary words are eliminated or better words than the ones used are substituted so that the best expression of thought and feelings are compressed within 17 syllables.

The following are some samples of the *haikus* our students have written:

Rain

Stormy night wet and cold
Haunted are houses
More haunted than before

BETTY BRITTON

Darkness and thunder
Sky of pigmented clouds
Drips colors of rainbow bright

BARRY IRWIN

Raindrops of the sky
Rain or dew out of the sky
Forms on grass that grows

GEORGE JARVIS

Halloween

Halloween costumes orange and black
Ring door bells
Scaring people

BETTY SMITH

Fear

Unknown darkness cries
And footsteps creeking
On stairways of old silence

BARRY IRWIN

Fear unknown danger
While mind sheeted in night's darkness
Is vigil

CAROL CUTHBERT

In the darkness of the night
On my way home
I saw an unknown person

ANNIE GRUM

Fear of the unknown
Anxiety of darkness
Terror of high places

CURTIS MONROE

64

I don't like the dark
I may have strange nightmares
I will be restless

                    MICHAEL FORD

Christmas

Time for Christmas train
Derailed from the mainline
To run down the mainline

                    COURTNEY BARRETT

Spring

Flowers grow when raindrops fall
Butterflies question
And the bee answers

                    RAYMOND HOLLOWAY

Spring is very refreshing
With the cool rain
Yet the leaves are falling

                    LIVINGSTON BRIZILL

Gentle are spring rains
Beautiful is it to be
Flowers of spring time

                    CURTIS MONROE

Confidence

She has the confidence
She uses some herself
And gives the rest away

                    LINDA SWINNEY

Dr. Friedman, the principal, Mr. Hurwitt, the assistant principal supervising the English department, and I would greatly appreciate an opportunity to learn how the writing of a *haiku* is taught in Japan. We would be most grateful for any assistance you may offer.

(Mrs.) Renee Cohen, English Teacher
Samuel Huntington Junior High School, J.H.S. 40, Queens
109-20 Union Hall St., Jamaica, 33, N.Y.

The Milieu of Haiku

Each *Haiku* is akin to
  Each flower we enjoy:
    Nice and lovely in itself

As the flower depends
  On the grace of Nature
    Permeating all good things

So *Haiku* depends much
  On the grace of *Milieu*
    Which is *Oriental Thought*

Two dews of this *Milieu*
  Are Confucian *Jen*
    And Buddhist *Zen*

These dews sparkle
  Under the sunbeams
    Of the all-forgiving love of God

God is the giver of all gifts
  Including even such things
    As dews, flowers and *Haiku*

The hint of *Haiku* is such
  That whatever has value
    Comes ultimately from God

Some people call it Nature
  But we call it the *Milieu*
    Where Love works universally

Jen and Zen, when scrutinized,
  Prove to be tender nieces
    Of Christian Love Divine

Love stresses sacrifice
  Jen stands for responsibility
    Zen implies indivisibility

These three are all one
  In the sense of taking
    The point of view of all mankind

Between *Haiku* and history
  Words and the world
    A one-to-infinity correspondence

Chapter II

Jen as a Way to Peace

The Art of being Good

A long look at the history of ethics shows the great lack of the art of being good. Too often did they stress the oughtness of the good. Thus a stern duty would characterize the moralist. People shy away from the rigor of the ethical teaching which is so exacting that we cannot put it into practice.

But ethic at its best is not obligatory in a grim sense. It is gratitude or appreciation. As Jesus would say it is spontaneous goodness. He referred to the flowers of the field. They would grow spontaneously as the warm season comes round. They come into a living harmony with the sun, the air, the lifegiving atmosphere of the spring-time, until they burst into shining radiance in the breeze. This is spontaneous. Human goodness at its noblest must be like that.

Confucian ethic is art itself. It is like a huge blossom, charming to look at, delightful to recall, purifying to the soul. It is as huge as the cosmos because the blossom of ethic derives nourishment from the law of Heaven itself. Heaven does not say much but causes the four seasons to recur.[1] The great attribute of Heaven and Earth is the giving and maintaining of life. Heaven overspreads all without partiality.[2] Earth sustains all without partiality. The sun and moon shine on all without partiality. Heaven produces the virtue in a true man. Without recognizing the ordinances of Heaven it is impossible to be a true man.

Ethic thus derived from Heaven aims to purify the inner life of the true man, relationships in home, school, office, state, world state, thus bringing about equality and peace in the international situation. Unlike Jesus Confucius saw no personal God in Heaven. But impartiality, equality, peace, life-giving, life-maintaining power was discerned in Heaven by Confucius whose ethic is a coherent unity of values on family, school, state, world state levels. This unity is so artistically framed that the cosmic blossom is the figure of speech apt to describe it. A young lady who knows how to smile amiably with big, liquid eyes would put powder on her face. This finishing touch of powdery charm is what Confucius would like to add to his own system of ethic.[3]

Confucius was a professional musician. He was able to play on stringed instruments well. He was a trained singer. He knew the theory of musicology, how group singing was to be conducted and how an orchestra should perform. He deemed music as an integral part of ethic. It should be both delightful and ennobling. Music is the blossoming of virtue.[4]

Good music stands for two things. An impressive, meaningful combination of sounds is one thing. An unforgettable finale or finishing-touch to this sound combination is the other. Confucian ethic is like that. Jen is the impressive, meaningful combination of ethical values, which transform the self, home, school, office, state, world state. Li is the unforgettable finale to the whole symphony of ethic. Jen is the ideal content of this ethic; Li its best form. Jen and Li are both artistic, academic, social, political, international, cosmological in the following sense. Ultimately they come from the benign structure of the cosmos. But they begin to be realized first in the inner life of the human self, then in the home, then in the school, office, state, world state. The combination of Jen and Li is of such a nature that it is like a tiny ripple created in the center of a lake by a pebble thrown into there. It spreads itself wider and wider until the whole lake comes under the influence of this ripple. In a way similar to this the whole world is bound to be the theatre of the influence of Jen and Li when a true man is the ruler of this world. Li is sometimes called decorum, propriety, ceremonies, or rituals.

Jen is such a lofty ideal, almost impossible to be realized

in any age. Confucius saw all this. Hence the following parable.

"A young man is in love with a young lady whose house is marked by the foliage of trees with large blossoms, looking as if they were beckoning to the man. He would like to call on her. But it is so far away that he does not dare to make the trip."[5] This is a parable Confucius tells his students that they may not use the loftiness of the Jen ideal as an excuse for not striving hard to realize it. If they are in love with Jen they can find the way to practice it. The main thing is for them continually to try to attain it. They should begin the task of world-remaking with the ennobling of their own inner lives.

Confucius knew artistic values rooted in the harmony of the cosmos are indispensable for political reform. Hence this conversation in a seminar. Student A said to the Master: "I like to rule over a country with a thousand carriages, situated between two strong neighbors, engaged in war and suffering from famine. If I become premier of that country, it would become orderly in three years." Here the Master smiled and said to Student B, "What is your ambition?" B said, "Let me have a small country. Put it in my charge. In three years the people would have enough to eat, but as for teaching them moral order or music I shall leave it to the superior man." The Master turned to Student C and asked, "How about you?" C answered, "At the ceremonies of the religious worship and at the conference of the princes, I should like to wear the ceremonial cap and gown. Thus I should be a minor official assisting at the ceremony." Here the Master spoke to Student D, "How about you?" D was playing on the *seh,* namely, a twenty-five-stringed instrument. But leaving the *seh,* he arose to speak. "You know my ambition is different from theirs." "It does not matter," said the Master, "We are trying to find out what each would like to do." Then he replied, "In late spring when the new spring dress is made, I would like to go with five or six grown-ups and six or seven children to bathe in a hot spring resort, and after the bath go to enjoy the breeze in the woods, and then sing on our

70

way home." The Master heaved a deep sigh and said, "You are the man after my own heart."[6] The meaning of this conversation is this. Confucius deems music, Jen, Li, as the most important virtue for any political reform, which is a desired result impossible to realize without Jen. The first three students were too superficially pragmatic. They had politics in mind; their teacher stood for ethical statesmanship rooted in Jen and Li.

Confucius derived his ethical insights from two classics, the *Book of Changes* and the *Book of Songs*. The *Book of Changes* contains the most profound cosmology in which human events were supposed to be rooted. It is this book which reveals to the superior man the ways in which the cosmos is full of harmony, impartiality, rhythm, symphony. This structure is what sustains life and the eternal principles of regularity and peace.

The *Book of Songs*[7] contains 305 odes and sacred anthems, besides 6 with music and title without texts. This book was edited by Confucius. There is one value which permeates the *Book of Songs*. That is spontaneity. All these odes and anthems are the spontaneous outburst of human emotion at its purest and noblest. This is the criterion which Confucius used as he collected and compiled them in book form. These songs inculcate how the superior man can regulate his inner life first, then his home, afterwards his state and the whole world. These songs can teach men many things. They can teach poetry, ethics, statesmanship, philosophy. They can teach customs, manners, and psychology as they ought to be. How to say and do the right thing at the right time, this too is taught by the *Book of Songs*.[8] If one studies all this and comes to understand how to put it into practice, he will be a first-class diplomat and statesman, as well as a superior man, knowing how to regulate himself. So thinking Confucius taught this book to all his students, especially his own son, Poyu.

Once a disciple of Confucius had a chance to ask Poyu frank questions. The first question was this. "You are the Master's own son. So you must get some special instruction

71

from your father." Poyu answered, "No, I do not receive any such treatment. Only when I walked past the hallway when my father stood there alone, he stopped me and asked me whether or not I had studied the *Book of Songs*. So I said that I had not. Then he said to me that without studying it I could not begin to talk sense. Some time later again I passed by the hallway where he stood alone. Once more he stopped me and asked, "Have you studied the *Book of Rites?*" So I said, "No." He said to me, "Without studying the *Book of Rites,* which explains the meaning of Li from the ethical, historical, cosmological points of view, one can never learn how to regulate his own inner life."[9] This disciple of his learned through this talk with Poyu three important things. The *Book of Songs* is worth studying. So is the *Book of Rites.* And the Master dealt with everyone, including his own son, with impartiality.

Confucius had a prized disciple to whom he married his lovely niece. The reason why this disciple was beloved is this. When his country was rightly governed he was entrusted with an important office. Even when it was lawless he did not lose his position. The secret for this was his habitual perusal of a chapter of the *Book of Songs,* in which this ode is found: "Here is a precious stone. If it has a flaw it can be polished that it may be flawless again. Here is a spoken word. If it is misleading nothing can make up for its bad effect."[10] Ethic is art. The *Book of Songs* teaches how to speak and how to be still. So Confucius would say to his students, "It inspires the soul, reveals the rise and fall of civilizations, makes us good mixers, teaches how tastefully to give expression to grievances."[11] At the age of 68 he returned to his own native country Lu in order to concentrate on the education of students and on the restoration of noble music and decorum. In this task he scored a shining success. During the last twenty-five centuries he has been the most influential leader in China's national life. The idol of countless millions of Chinese youth has been this schoolmaster, not a military hero or a messiah.[12] A sophisticated intellectual like Bertrand

Russell thinks of Confucian ethic as the most fruitful means by which to bring about global amity and peace.[13] The uniqueness of this ethic lies in its artistic appeal rooted in the grandeur of the natural world. Heaven is still. But the four seasons recur. The rhythm of the many-hued cosmos is effective with its unspeakable beauty. Man should emulate this charming impartiality, thus bringing about the ethical flower of benign cooperation.

"One should know how to look kind,"[14] said Confucius to a student of his, in answer to a question on filial piety. Filial piety means many things. If there is hard work to be done in the home, the son should do it without causing the old parent any anxiety. Tasty dishes should be offered to the parent. But this is not enough. The son, doing the hard task and offering the delicacies, should appear benign. His whole attitude is even more important. Ethic is not confined to deed alone. The way it is done should be aesthetically fine. It must be full of grace and charm. Confucius stresses this artistic side of it more than any other men I know.

The westerner is apt to be utilitarian, pragmatic, crude. He yawns, becomes easily offended, boisterous. Japan has become westernized ethically too. Do not America and Japan need to learn from the ethic of artistic effectiveness? A former student of mine lives in Hongkong, China. She is now a wife to a successful Chinese lawyer. Graduating from a Tokyo university she was a stewardess of a British air line. She was grace and charm personified, way up in the air, rendering services to passengers of all nationalities in a precarious situation nearer to the seventh heaven, where they would be more susceptible to the kindness of this angelic being. Not argument but appreciation is needed to counteract the accumulated prejudice against foreign countries in the hearts of these passengers. This Japanese stewardess did her work well. Today she is happy in her new home in Hongkong with her Chinese husband. I would like to have attended their wedding ceremony. Even this very moment I would like to call on them and talk with them about Confucian ethic once again.

It takes appreciation to change the divided world.

Art looks spontaneous. But feel the unassuming work which is behind it. "The superior man is painstaking and thoroughgoing in getting ready for each art of graciousness. He is minute and careful in exerting himself. And yet, despite all this care and preparation on his part, he appears to be amiable, joyous, exhilarated."[15] He is so attractive as to invite the most taciturn to come and talk to him. This is artistic goodness. There is no outward sign of toil there. Only ease, comfort, relaxation.

Once his students were curious. They wondered how Confucius would look like in his own home. Calling on him they found him calm and smiling. This is what *Analects* 151 says, making many of my friends like him. Goodness is not irritable. It is radiant, hoping all things. It is soft and yet strong because it is one with the life-giving grace of the universe, which looks almost sleepy but moves the stars and galaxies.

As if to illustrate this highest level of goodness, Confucius referred to a splendid horse, which is characterized not so much by the fact of running 1,000 li a day as by that of being free from a bad temper.[16] Not power but poise, not strength but soft-heartedness, not push but peace is the way out of the troubled world which is full of grievances, vindictiveness, fear of total war. War is terribly destructive. The art of peace-making is urgently needed. The West is too set in thinking of gaining power and a balance of power. The wisdom of the East must be incorporated into all levels of life, especially political and international levels.

Ethic as an art has another hint to make. Art means exquisiteness. It is the more elaborate part of life. It means not merely living and dying but going through them all with rare skill and keen appreciation. When one method of doing things fails, another method, more unusual and painstaking, is thought of. When blue does not work pink is applied. When a positive practicing of goodwill fails, a negative way is devised. The West says, "Do to others what you would like to have them do to you." This is straight-forward. But suppose I do to you what I enjoy but you do not. The result would not be good. So the East says. "Do not do to others what you would not like to have them do to you."[17] The result might be better. I like raw fish but you do not. So I should not ask you to eat raw fish. Often I do not know exactly what you wish. Even the frankest Westerner is never completely frank. So I should be reticent sometimes. Otherwise what I would do to you may be annoying or patronizing. What I am thinking of offering you may be a new ethic, a strange philosophy, or a religion unreasonable to you. Then I must be especially careful. Here I am pleading for more humility and less dogmatism. True, sometimes I must give my child what she does not like to take, say, a bitter pill. So it is dangerous to generalize and say that the Eastern way which is Confucian is always better. It is safe to say, however, that we would like to have more methods because our problem is manysided. Both West and East should put their heads together. If a man is not able to do something a lady should be asked to do it, as in the case of cooking or nursing a baby. If all men advocate non-pacifism at least women should be all pacifists.

The art of wholesome self-enjoyment is part of Confucian ethic. Effortless appreciation is sometimes needed by all of us. True, effortful participation is needed too. And the West is good in stressing this active virtue. But as the day is followed by the night, so work must be followed by rest. Confucius tasted deeply the joy of singing, playing on a stringed instrument, having a reunion with a friend, reviewing a book after a period of time, delighting in the hues and hums of natural phenomena. He knew how to enjoy himself, doing nothing when he was alone. The West is too busy, finding fault with the status quo, changing it without knowing that such a change may be a change for the worse, obtaining power in order to mistreat it because human nature is such that anyone having power over others will be sure to abuse it. Ethic as an art is the enjoyment of opening our spiritual eyes of appreciation. It is the art of doing nothing in the way of gaining too much power over others. It is the secret of true happiness. It is also the art of being free from becoming enslaved to the excess ambition to lord it over other men and nations. Our nuclear age needs this ethic.

The ethic of power means to dominate, influence, use others. The ethic of art means to appreciate, respect, honor others. "You may deprive an army of its commander but cannot deprive even the meanest soldier of his will."[18] For the West the word positive has a good connotation. But the East differs here. Not aggressiveness but reserve or reticence is preferred. To be meddlesome is a vice for the Easterner. Chinamen and Hindus have been behaving themselves well, both individually and nationally. But the West has been the chief invader of Asia and Africa. It is really the East, with the exception of westernized Japan, which is entitled to inherit the world. Christ is right: The meek will inherit the earth. It is ironical that not the West with the Beatitudes but the East with the Analects has been a peace-maker in history.

. . . . . .

Art is self-evident: immediate enjoyment of the whole pattern. It has no painful clash between parts. Jen sees no clash between individual and social ethics, between motive and result, between ethic and aesthetics. It is spontaneous, not strained; delightful, not didactic; inspiring, not inhibiting; ennobling, devoid of vulgarity; convincing, not confusing; effortless, not effortful. It is modeled after Heaven at its most rhythmic, impartial, equalitarian, peaceful. It is to ennoble raw human nature.

Beauty is a brighter, clearer, more vivid, more exquisite, more hopeful side of life. It is not a darker, more uncertain, troublesome, hopeless, sinful, destructive, paradoxical side of it. Jen would ask the world to dwell on the more constructive side of each situation in life. Heavenly dreams do come true in history. Encouraged by past prayer the world should bestir itself in order to bring future fruit. Realistic optimism is better than morbid pessimism. Peace is not a hopeless dream. In our task of peace-making we have Heaven and History to fall back on. Jesus saw a personal God, the Lord of Heaven and

76

Earth,[19] the Father of all mankind. Confucius saw a quasi-personal Heaven, impartial and rhythmic, reminding us of the God of contemporary scientists like Hermann Weyl:[20] the Harmony of Harmonies,[21] the Ultimate Source of concretions or concrescences, ethical, aesthetical, cosmic.

Home Nurtures the Good

Confucius was an able statesman. In the fourteenth year of Duke Ting (496 B.C.), he was fifty-six years old. In that year he was promoted to the position of the Chief Minister.[22] He had done remarkably well as the Grand Secretary of Justice. Hence this promotion. After three months of his premiership, things lost on the streets were not stolen, and foreigners visiting the country did not have to go to the police, but came to Lu like a country of their own. He was concerned about all men as brothers under Heaven. He was good not only to his own country but to all other countries as well. His was a global concern. All the seas of the world proved to be internally connected with one another. Under the banner of decorum there was no national barrier. All humanity enjoying peace, equality, Li and Jen was his vision.

This cosmopolitan amity of his, however, had its root in every home where parents and brothers and sisters live together. We may not have international peace but we can have a home, well ordered and regulated. A shining vision is needed. A noble ideal helps. But what we do here and now counts too. Be a good member of the family. Here under the shelter of the home nurture such values as filial piety, brotherly love, mutual help, sacrifice, endurance, moral stamina, vicarious joy and suffering. Confucius stressed filial piety as a symbol of the good, because this is not what children practice in all homes universally. Many a scholar or a social reformer is a poor son in his own home. He who is not a good son in his family cannot be expected to be a good premier, diplomat, internationalist. Confucius knew this. It is hard to say which is more difficult to realize, filial piety or international amity?

In a way the former is more difficult to practice because sons and their parents are together most of the time, whereas foreigners do not have to be dealt with always. If a son is good toward his own parents, for a long period of time, he must have some unusual excellence, which is most likely to be transmuted into a new value like interracial amity when an opportunity offers itself. Filial piety means for a person to be ethical in the right way, at the right time, and in the right place. If this ethic is mastered all other values will most likely be realized in due time. It is the first and most crucial test of moral character. So thinking Confucius stressed filial piety as the most representative ethical value under the sun. "A son who is faithful to his parents and brothers is apt to be a good citizen of the state. A superior man works on the fundamentals of ethic. When that is fixed the higher structure of the good will be ready to be erected. The fundamentals of Jen are filial piety and brotherly concern."[23]

It may be better for me to use a figure of speech different from that which I have mentioned above. I think of many concentric circles, the innermost of which is the self, surrounded by the home, school, state, world state, which is the largest, outermost concentric circle, with the exception of Heaven. Heaven differs from all these concentric circles in that it is boundless. It is not a circle but is infinite. Among all these circles and Heaven there is a two-way traffic. Heaven is the ultimate giver and sustainer of all the values to be realized in the self, home, school, state, world state. At the same time the self must take the initiative, humanly speaking, that it may be regulated first, then home, school, state, world state should be regulated one after another, in that order. This is the centrifugal movement of filial piety. And that should be inspired by the creativity of Heaven. This is the centripetal activity of Li. When these concentric circles are regulated Jen is realized. It is the consummation of filial piety and Li. Heaven-initiated and self-initiated, Confucian ethic is fulfilled in Jen. Jen is as infinite as Heaven and can be enshrined in the self of the superior man, home, school, state, world.

Confucius achieved much as prime minister. He achieved even more as president of a flourishing university where 3,000 able scholars studied. Even after his death this school continued to flourish. During the past 25 centuries the *Analects* continued to be the best-seller in the East. The ideal personality of the Chinese people has always been a scholar like Confucius.

What does study mean for Confucius? It is a way to Jen. "Study widely, have the strong will to put into practice what you have studied, ask questions whenever they arise, think pragmatically that your study may be applied to problems which are round about you, then you are on the way to Jen."[24] "If a man loves kindness, but does not love study, he will be ignorant. If he loves wisdom but does not love study, he will upset things. If he loves simplicity but does not love study, he will be stale. If he loves courage and does not love study, he will be unruly. If he loves decisiveness and does not love study, he will be stubborn."[25]

By study Confucius meant two things. The first is the classics like the *Book of Songs,* the *Book of Changes,* and the *Book of Rites.* These classics were indispensable because they teach Li, Jen, History, Heaven. After his death, *Spring and Autumn,*[26] written by Confucius, a chronicle of events of two and half centuries, 722-481 B.C., *Analects, Central Harmony,* recorded sayings of Confucius and his disciples, *Mencius*[27] too were included as classics worthy to be studied with respect and endearment.

And yet the subject of study is much wider in meaning. According to Confucius, "Study without thought is vague; thought without study is dangerous."[28] And thought means any self-examination; doubting, comparative scrutiny. This reminds me of Tennyson who urges us

"To follow knowledge like a sinking star

Beyond the utmost bounds of human thought."[29]

It makes me think of a French thinker who would advise the

student to doubt where people naively take things for granted. Doubt when others feel no impulse to doubt, then you will be creative. This is in keeping with the spirit of modern science and mathematics. In Confucius we see a rare combination of a respect for classics and an urge for creative self-examination. "Study the past, understand the new, then you will be good enough to teach."[30] Here is revealed a fine interchange of classical scholarship and freedom of thought. But Confucius himself stressed the importance of study more than freedom of thought, whereas contemporary Chinese philosophers and scientists seem to put a greater emphasis on freedom of thought. Once Confucius exercised freedom of thought all day but did not gain much. So he switched to study. The ways the student should study are three. The first is the way of knowing. The second way is that of liking. The third is the way of enjoying heartily. The first is not so good as the second, which is not so good as the third.[31]

His class was something like a seminar in a modern American graduate school. Only a few students sat with him. One of the students would look courteous. A second would be happy. A third would play on a twenty-five-stringed musical instrument that a soothing atmosphere might be enjoyed by the whole class. And in this delightful milieu a give and take of ideas was conducted. The teacher knew each of the students so well that what that student needed in particular was given him by the Master. A fool-hardy student was taught to be careful. A retiring and hesitant student was led to be courageous and adventurous. A student like Yen Huei who thoroughly enjoyed study was praised and encouraged. A student who was too eager to seek employment was taught to be like Yen Huei, who enjoyed study for its own sake.

A student must study the lesson before he comes to class. He must study it without the help of the teacher until he comes to say within himself, "What does it mean? What should be the right interpretation of it? What must I do?"[32] Confucius would say this kind of inquiry is necessary before the classroom work actually begins. He would not teach the student

80

unless the latter had made his preparation well until he had become indignant because of his own slowness of comprehension and had twisted his lips in disgust and irritation. One's study is sometimes hard. But like any great value in life study is a mixture of hardship and joy, suffering and delight. So the *Analects* begins with the impressive summary of one's experience of study, "Confucius said, 'Study and after a while review, is that not exhilarating?' "[33]

Let us ask ourselves this question "Today do students study? Do instructors study?" An amazing number of schools there are in countries like America and Japan. Many instructors and students merely get by without exerting themselves too much. They are not painstaking in their work. They do not go the second mile. They do not do excellent work. They shy away from the most laborious task of making the best preparation beforehand and of reviewing their lessons afterwards. Their work is mercenary and perfunctory. So there is no inspiration in class, in the campus life. Education is like a fog. When students are in the midst of it it is nothing charming. Its charm is seen only after they graduate, when they look back upon their school life from a distance. Then it is like a heavenly cloud, shining with the brilliance of the setting[34] sun. Too late. Would not a little Confucian advice breathe inspiration into our campus life today?

The Ethic of the State

Confucius was a first-class statesman. If his native country Lu had respected his judgment it would have become an ideal state. Unfortunately something happened to prevent him from finishing his task of remaking Lu and the whole Chinese Continent.

The people of Ch'i, Lu's neighboring state, heard wonderful things going on in Lu under his premiership and said, "If Confucius remains in power in Lu, Lu will become so strong and we being the nearest neighbor would be the first to be dominated." They selected eighty of the most charming girls of the country. They were presented together with a hundred and twenty fine horses to the Ruler of Lu, who was much enchanted with them, and he did not attend to his duties.[35] The sex appeal of those voluptuous girls was preferred to the world-remaking wisdom of the premier.

This is what happened in 496 B.C. Something similar to this has happened in history since then. Here is a problem to which our age must be attentive. A tension between pleasure and wisdom is an ever recurring problem for all of us today. Then what is his wisdom in the field of statesmanship? This must be explained here.

His wisdom is simply self-criticism. It is a penetrating self-examination on the part of the ruler himself. He who has the power to govern the whole people is asked to illumine his own inner life with the light of candid self-criticism. This self-criticism is based on Jen which says that the ruler should take the whole responsibility for the welfare of the people. When things go well the people should get credit for it. When things go wrong he should be held responsible for all that. This ideal of Jen-statesmanship is unique in the history of mankind. In other words, the sin of all the people is ascribed to the ruler alone. And his sin is his alone, no one else's. This statesmanship is in line with the spirit of Heaven. So the ruler is called the Son of Heaven. He should know how to use the people during the season when they are not busy with their own work on the farm. He should use them for the right cause and in the right way. He should see to it that the rivers should be under control and that floods may not cause any trouble. This aspiration appeals to the Japanese people today because in Japan floods, tidal waves, mountain slides cause casualties each year. Also food, justice, peace, equality were what the ruler was responsible for. Weights and measures must be rightly regulated. Decorum, music, law must be adjusted too. The ruler must be generous, forgiving, trustworthy, keen, alert, fair.[36]

Confucius claims the realizability of this statesmanship. He refers to the first three Jen-minded rulers of the Chinese people.

Yao, Shun, Wu. Some say they are legendary figures. But this does not dispute the fact that ideal of Jencracy is adumbrated in the *Analects* just the same, thus urging us to think about it, learn from it, profit by it. It is an impossible ideal like Christian love, Buddhist compassion, democracy. It has never been realized fully anywhere. But just the same it is valuable as an ideal. We need it to counteract all the evil forces at work within and round about us. And there is always a possibility of improving the status quo in accordance with such an ideal. It purifies and ennobles the task before us. And historical experience cannot dispute the possibility as such.

Confucius further explains the ideal of Jen as what Wu practiced. Wu was flawless, in economizing his own expense for food, clothing and shelter, thus spending more money on the ceremony of ancestor-worship, on strengthening river banks.[37] The Jen-minded ruler is very careful as to what cause the people are used for, thus winning their hearts whole-heartedly. The ruler spares every possible item of unnecessary expense, making the people as well-fed as possible.[38] Confucius would say that the true worry of a state is not in a foreign nation but within the hedges of its own ruler's palace, not in scarcity but in inequality, not in poverty but in dissatisfaction.[39] The right use of the people would be for the ruler to take the initiative in working for them. When they have done good work he should amply reward them for their services. And in rewarding them he should be prompt and never be tired of doing so.[40] The ruler should know that it takes time to reform society. Even the best ruler would have to spend at least thirty years to do any basic work in the improvement of society. During all that time he must be patient, continuing to do his work assiduously.

Confucius is an Oriental who has a highly artistic temperament. When he said one thing he means that that has a hidden dimension which is more important than what he refers to on the surface. For instance, he referred to the Jen-minded ruler. But here he implied that every one was to aspire to be Jen-minded. It is true that there can be only one ruler. And yet every member of his state can cooperate with this ruler. The best thing this citizen can do would be for him to become Jen-minded himself, thus being the best helper of the ruler. So this is what Confucius meant when he said, "The student must be high-minded for his burden is heavy and his journey is long. Humanity is the burden he imposes upon his own shoulders. Is that not a heavy burden? Only death would put an end to his journey. Is that not a long journey?"[41]

This sense of the responsibility of the individual has been a source of inspiration to many students of Confucian statesmanship. This has taught a Chinese patriot of the seventeenth century, Ku Yen-wu, to write, "Even the humblest citizen has a share in the responsibility for the prosperity or the downfall of the empire."[42]

This sense of responsibility goes with that of dignity. A good man is he who cannot be cowed by shame and lowliness, who cannot be bent by power and threat. Further, moral responsibility goes with the duty to fight misrule, corruption, unrighteousness. Thus it has become a tradition for Chinese scholars to fight against tyrannical monarchs in the interest of the people. From this stems China's fight for freedom. Jencracy goes with democracy. Both aim at the same welfare of the people ultimately. Only the former begins to work from within the scholar or ruler, whereas the latter begins to do its work from the side of the people. Thus Jencracy is centrifugal; democracy is centripetal. China would say something more than this. Democracy without the inspiration of Jencracy will never achieve its aim. The former is legalistic and external; the latter spiritual and internal.

In the *Book of Filial Piety*, which is a later essay by a Han scholar, Confucius is made to say something revolutionary. It is the duty of the son to fight it out before his father who is not righteous. Likewise a minister should fight it out before his sovereign who is bad. This Confucian contention is followed up by Mencius. "If a ruler treats his subjects like grass or dirt, they will treat him like a bandit or an enemy."[43]

Confucius did not believe in indiscriminate goodwill. He did not advocate the principle of returning good for evil. He would say, "Return justice for injustice, and good for good." The idea of returning good for evil was taught by the Taoist. Thus the Taoist is like a liberal American Christian like Harry Emerson Fosdick[44] who believes in the hidden moral possibilities of any man, even a sinner whose mental mannerisms have already been fixed. Fosdick would see in adults, whom society has sized up, shining possibilities of future growth. The difference between Confucius and Niebuhr[45] is just this. The former is an artist, appreciating aesthetic values thought of as stemming from the harmony and rhythm of Heaven itself, whereas the latter's appreciation of beauty is more or less confined to the perceptual loveliness of nature. Both are weak in physical science.

According to Confucius, music expresses the harmony[46] of the universe; while rituals the order of the universe. The wise ruler tries to guide the people's ideals and aspirations by means of rituals, establish harmony in sounds by means of music, regulate conduct by means of government, and prevent immorality by means of punishments. Ritualism, music, punishment, government have a common goal, which is to bring about unity in the people's hearts and carry out the principles of political order.

When a man becomes materialistic the principle of reason in Nature is missed and man is a slave of his own lower desires. Then arises cunning, deceit, disobedience. Then the strong bully the weak, the majority persecute the minority, the clever deceive the simple-minded, the strong exploit the weak, the helpless become neglected.

Music rises from Heaven, while rituals are patterned on the Earth. In order to have the proper music and rituals we must know the principles of Heaven and Earth. To be in harmony with these patterns would result in peace and order. The parents and children are loving toward one another, the juniors respect the elders and this respect is extended to all people and the ruler lives a harmonious, gracious life, then the harmony of Heaven and the order of Earth will prevail in the state. Without this harmony and order the peace of the state will not come. Inspiring music shares the rhythm of the cosmos. Fine rituals share the order of the cosmos. This music would teach men to aspire to love one another. This ritualism would cause them to live piety. Noble music stands for the primordial forces of the cosmos. Ritualism which is orderly reflects the creative gradations of the cosmos. Here Confucian music reminds us of the Primordial Nature of God in the cosmology of A. N. Whitehead;[47] Confucian ritualism of the Consequent Nature of God in the same cosmology. Confucius is prescientific and Whitehead is a sophisticated mathematician. But both have a cosmic intuition which is penetrating in its aesthetic depth. Both make an aesthetic order the ultimate basis[48] of everything that exists in this charming universe.

The sage contemplates the clear mandates of Heaven. Thus he traces things from their beginning and follows them to their end. Thus he knows what can be said of death and life. As the *Book of Songs* has it, "The twittering yellow bird alights on a little mound."[49] When the bird rests, it knows where to rest. Should a human being be inferior to a bird in knowing where to rest or dwell in? The *Book of Songs* again says, "How dignified and inspiring was King Weh! He was careful in choosing that which he should dwell in."[50] The ruler dwells in benevolence. The minister dwells in respectfulness. The son dwells in filial piety. The father dwells in kindness.

The *Book of Songs* says, "Look at that curve in the River of Ch'i. How green are the bamboos there! Here is our prince. He looks like a piece of jade, chiseled and polished."[51] Thus the perfection of the prince's character is praised. It is akin to the perfection of the grandeur of nature!

World Peace

The restoration of peace in the world depends on ordering the national life. When those in authority respect the old people, common folk learn to be good sons. When those in authority respect their superiors, common folk become humble and respectful. When those in authority show kindness to the young, helpless common folk do likewise. Thus the sage has a principle with which, as with a measuring square, he may regulate his conduct. Jen showing itself in infinite kindness and courtesy is it.

Suppose a man dislikes something in his superiors. He should not show that in his dealings with his inferiors. Suppose a man dislikes something in his inferiors. He should not show that in his own dealings with his superiors. What he dislikes in those in front of him, let him not display toward those behind. The *Book of Songs,* says, "How the people are pleased with their ruler, who is like a parent to the people."[52]

If one nation is just and fair in dealing with another nation in accordance with the principle that what one would not like to have another do to him that he should not do to him, then these two nations will be on friendly terms. If all the nations of all the world become friendly to one another in line with the same principle, world peace will come. As Confucius says, "If you are courteous and respectful toward another, all men in all the world will be brothers."[53]

Confucius is a champion of equality. If one nation enjoys a higher standard of living than others, there will be much dissatisfaction in the latter. This is against the ideal of equality. We should be more afraid of inequality than of scarcity or poverty. Here he says something which is profoundly suggestive. It is applicable to the international situation in which we are today. If one nation or two nations are much wealthier than others, this inequality causes dissatisfaction, fear, hatred, envy, jealousy. And world peace will be endangered sooner or later.

The wisdom of Confucius is shown in the tension between the first best and the second best. His first best is a vision of the *Great Common Wealth, tat'ung. Ta* means "great" and *t'ung* means "common", according to the tenth chapter of the *Book of Rites.* This is a Confucian Utopia where none of the humanistic distinctions in *Li* would be needed. It is a realm of perfect equality and impartiality like Heaven, which is full of harmony and rhythm. This was realized only in the dynasties of the first three emperors.

The second best is the best social order found in the world today. Between this and the utopia there is a big difference. So a sincere attempt must be made to lift the present order up to the highest. This attempt is to be made and at the same time the present order must be accepted with a certain sense of resignation. Otherwise too much impatience or dissatisfaction would be caused in the hearts of social reformers. A continuous zeal for further reform coupled with this sense of resignation would characterize the true man. Dr. Sun Yat Sen is an example of this combination.[54]

Dr. Sun like Confucius was, for a long time, a frustrated wanderer in foreign countries, thus learning how to view things from the point of view of an estranged member of a minority group. Hence his insight into longings of the poignant stranger, whose prophetic challenge to the privileged class is rich in visions needed for social reform. That is in line with the ethic of Mo-tzu,[55] c. 479-c.381, who stressed the political urgency of listening to utterances by members of a despised and neglected class in society. Unlike Marx he hopes to retain values in the old world, the structure of which must be changed from time to time. But reform must be devoid of war. As Mencius stressed there is no just war in history. This should be more emphatically stated today when war has reached the peaks of destructive dangerousness.

REFERENCES

Chapter II

1. Shigeto Hozumi, **The Analects of Confucius Interpreted Anew,** passage 450, p. 514. Shakai Kyoiku Kyokai, Tokyo, 1949.
2. **Chinese Philosophy,** p. 10, The Peter Pauper Press, New York, translated by Lionel Giles.
3. **The Analects of Confucius,** passage 48.
4. Lin Yutang, **The Wisdom of Confucius,** p. 251-272, The Modern Library, New York, 1938. **Chinese Philosophy,** p. 70.
5. **Analects,** passage 235.
6. **Ibid.,** 278.
7. **The Wisdom of Confucius,** p. 40.
8. Shigeki Kaizuka, **Confucius,** p. 69, 70, Iwanami Shoten, Tokyo, 1951. **Analects,** passages 18, 192, 258, 307, 430, 440, 441.
9. **Analects,** passage 430.
10. **Ibid.,** 258.
11. **Ibid.,** 440.
12. **China,** edited by H. F. MacNair, p. 223, University of California Press, 1951.
13. Bertrand Russell, **Sceptical Essays,** p. 97-108, George Allen & Unwin, London, 1935.
14. **Analects,** pasage 24.
15. **Ibid.,** 330.
16. **Ibid.,** 365.
17. **Ibid.,** 280, 399.
18. **Ibid.,** 230.
19. Matthew 11:25.
20. Hermann Weyl, **Symmetry,** Princeton University Press, 1952.
21. A. N. Whitehead, **Adventures of Ideas,** p. 376, Macmillan, New York, 1933.
22. **The Wisdom of Confucius,** p. 66.
23. **Analects,** passage 2.
24. **Ibid.,** 474.
25. **Ibid.,** 439.
26. Lin Yutang attributes it to Confucius but this is refuted by scholars like Saukichi Tsuda, **A Study of Confucianism,** volume I, p. 4, Iwanami Shoten, Tokyo, 1950.**The Wisdom of Confucius,** p. 4.
27. Mencius is a book of recorded teachings of Mencius, 372-289 B.C. who ranks next to Confucius in The Confucian Temples and stands for Confucian moral idealism. Lin Yutang, **The Wisdom of Confucius,** viii, p. 273-290.

28. Analects, passage 31.
29. Tennyson, Ulysses.
30. Analects, passage 27.
31. Ibid., 137.
32. Ibid., 155.
33. Ibid., 1.
34. Cf. A. N. Whitehead, Essays in Science and Philosophy, p. 126, Philosophical Library, New York, 1948.
35. The Wisdom of Confucius, p. 67.
36. Analects, 337, 494.
37. Ibid., 205.
38. Ibid., 5.
39. Ibid., 418.
40. Ibid., 191.
41. China, p. 224.
42. The Wisdom of Confucius, p. 41.
43. Mencius, chapter 92.
44. H. E. Fosdick, Adventurous Religion, p. 33-44, Blue Ribbon Books, New York, 1926.
45. Reinhold Niebuhr, An Interpretation of Christian Ethics, chapter 6. Harper & Brothers Publishers, New York, 1935.
46. A. N. Whitehead, Process and Reality, p. 524. The Social Science Book Store, New York, 1929. The Wisdom of Confucius, p. 260.
47. A. N. Whitehead, Religion in the Making, p. 91, Cambridge at the University Press, 1927. Whitehead says that God is the myriad-faceted mirror which discloses to every creature its own inherent greatness. p. 139. Confucius would say that Heaven is the multi-colored mirror which reveals to every man his own potential worth, which is Jen.
48. The Wisdom of Confucius, p. 142.
49. Ibid.
50. Ibid.
51. Ibid.
52. Analects, 283.
53. The Wisdom of Confucius, p. 225.
54. Michio Iwamura, San Min Chu I and Modern China, Iwanami Shoten, Tokyo, 1949.
55. Fung Yu-Lan, A History of Chinese Philosophy, Chapter V., Princeton University Press, 1952; Shigeki Kaizuka, Shoshi Hyakka, "Many Masters and Hundred Schools", Chapter II, Iwanami Shoten, Tokyo, 1961. Cf. The Confucian Persuasion, edited by Arthur F. Wright, Stanford University Press, 1960; Confucianism in Action, edited by David S. Nivison and Arthur F. Wright, Stanford University Press, 1959.

90

Chapter III

Zen as a Way to Peace

The Song of Zen

The leafy arbors
  Of Indian woods
    Are highly enticing

There clear-eyed sages
  Would listen to
    The humming of streams

Many-hued, multi-voiced
  Is the natural orchestra
    Making music, noble and clear

White birds, peacocks,
  Singing in blessed bowers,
    Chanting the hymn of peace

It is the song
  Of exhilaration
    Over the highest bliss

Now we must listen
  Fully to comprehend
    The meaning of Zen

It is rebirth,
  Health, joy, truth,
    And lasting peace

Let us hear it
  That we all may
    Examine this way to peace

Zen

Dream is often more beautiful than real life. This is especially true of India. She has been invaded[1] by foreigners many times, subjugated by them, thus undergoing all kinds of pain, shame, suffering. And yet she has continued to sing a song, dream a dream, uphold a vision, saying that the whole world is one and that even our most staunch, irreconcilable enemy is a part of the big unity of which we ourselves are members. The dream of the Indian thinker can be epitomized by a seventeen-syllabled *haiku* which I composed last spring:

How noble and sublime	*Ara toto*
To see one's own self	*Tekini wagamio*
In the proudest enemy	*Miru kokoro*

The West says, "Love your enemy." India says, "There is no enemy," "All men are part of a large unity of which we and the enemy are members."

All this sounds strange and fantastic. It sounds like a kind of sophistry in a world where division, tension, enmity, war stand out. The dream India dreams, however, cannot be brushed aside as a mere phantasm. It is not a story based on the testimony of sight, but an insight into a more profound dimension of the world. It is akin to Christian love, in terms of which there is neither East nor West, neither Jew nor Gentile, neither white nor colored. This love is not practiced always and everywhere in the West, but its value and truth is never doubted for a moment. Likewise the dream about a vast unity of which all men and all things are integral parts claims to have a similar value and validity. If its truth is believed firmly, causing all men to realize their potential interwovenness into one unity, their world would be actually transformed into that of lasting peace, universal brotherhood, supreme bliss. Is this claim true? Is there a sense in which our world has another dimension of interwovenness other than that of discreteness, strife, cacophony?

92

These days people in the West talk about Zen a great deal, without seeing all its meaning. But the Indian insight into universal interwovenness is at least a facet of the truth revealed to the human mind through the kind of experience which is called Zen. Zen, samādhi,[2] or dhyāna,[3] means "deep thought of life and death." This thought is to engender the interwovenness of all entities, including men, animals, inanimate things, the rest of the wide universe. If this interwovenness is true, then all men and all things are actually my fellow-members of the vast unity, which is this universe. Thus it is natural and reasonable for me to come to think of them with a newly awakened love. This love should be just as real and vital as my love of myself. That is why Zen is to enkindle a world-wide love of all men and all things. There should be no difference in meaning and intensity between my self-love and my love of all men and things. I cannot exist without the cosmic support in which I am rooted. And men, including my enemy, are part of the cosmos which sustains me.

True, various Zen masters have interpreted the meaning of Zen in various ways. But what I have said about Zen is fundamental. And here I would like to trace the history of Zen back to the pre-Buddhist days, when the aborigines of India used to withdraw into the primeval forest to meditate on the destiny of the human soul. The colorful hermitages[4] of the Indian forest must have been beautiful and inspiring. World-weary men would be consoled by the hues and hums of the foliage, the music of streams, birds and the charm of the whole atmosphere of natural phenomena. There those thinkers watched and wondered. The leafy avenues within the forest were both inviting and inspiring, giving those thinkers chance to wander peacefully through them, hit upon unprecedented ideas, burst forth into triumphant hallelujahs. This is Zen in its primitive form. It means a close contact of the human soul with the cosmic context. This communion is achieved by means of a quiet meditation on the part of the thinking mind to solve the spiritual problems it faces through a cosmic insight into the meaning of the higher destiny of its eternal pilgrimage.

This enlightenment due to quiet thought is the earmark of the tradition of the Indian people. It existed before the Aryans came invading in the thirteenth century before Christ. This invasion has a vital meaning in remoulding the content of Zen and has to be understood sympathetically.

The Aryans used to live in the area in Europe which is to the north of Caucasus. They were a nomadic people. In the thirteenth century before Christ they became divided into two groups, one of which went into the area which is northern Europe today. The other group came down south into the northwestern part of India. They were tall, blonde, strong, intelligent, conquering the dark, small aborigines of India. For some time bloody, cruel conflicts continued until at last the invaders came to control the new Continent, framing the upper stratum of society, whereas the vanquished became its lower class of serfs.

The great problem of India in those days, after the actual fighting was over was this: How can the conquerors live peacefully with the vanquished in the same continent? This was a big racial need of theirs. To go with it was another need which had to be met by the inhabitants of India. That was a religious, philosophical need of reconciling the myriad deities they believed into one world-principle. Some explanation is necessary so that the reader may see the depth and dimension of this new task.

By 1000 B. C. the Indo-Aryans had established their sacred scripture, namely, the Rig-Veda.[5] This was to show the Hindus how to heal the spiritual wounds of the vanquished, which had been caused by the Aryan invasion and the skirmishes which ensued. The religion of the Rig-Veda is not simple. It refers to many deities functioning in the universe. Heaven-God, Sun-God, Dawn-crimson-God, Thunder-God, Rain-God, and some three thousand other deities representing impressive and beneficent phenomena in the natural world, presided over the wide universe.

In this polytheistic atmosphere of the Rig-Veda we can discern an attempt to trace all things back to a world-principle, thus explaining coherently the multi-dimensional doings of Nature and men. Here the problem is a religious, cosmological one of seeing underneath the multiplicity of the world some coherent unity on the part of one world-principle, functioning in all these myriad deities. The only possible way of realizing this philosophical aspiration is one of seeing interwovenness among many wills and functions on the part of the deities. They are varied on the surface but deep down, underneath the surface, those are interdependent, thus fulfilling one ultimate purpose to be achieved in the course of the world process. Here we see the manifestation of the Hindu genius to reconcile diversities into a functional unity. Interdependence among them is logically possible only when it is interwovenness in a metaphysical sense. That means that ultimately there is only one coherent whole, which appears to be diversified on the surface. What is affirmed here is twofold: the surface manyness and deeper oneness. These two truths are affirmed simultaneously.

Later many Upanishads, namely philosophical appendices to the Veda, were written. The Sanskrit word, Upanishad, means "sitting closely together," or "secret conversation." This implies the authority of the Veda, which the free thinker examined from the point of view of its relation to actual experiences on the part of mankind. So this free examination is in line with the more philosophical part of the Rig-Veda. Between 650 B.C. and 200 A.D. thirteen Upanishads were written.[6] The main philosophy which runs through these thirteen principal Upanishads is a pan-psychic view which explains all things in terms of the identity of Atman-Brahman. Atman is the minutest entity of the world, namely, the human soul. This is a spiritual counterpart of the Greek concept of the atom, which is a material "uncut", in terms of which the ancient Greeks tried to explain the natural world. Brahman is the vastest whole, namely, the entire universe interpreted in terms of the coherent unity of all kinds of Atman. Atman is infinitely small. But it mirrors the entire universe which is Brahman. Atman attains its enlightenment by its relation to

95

Brahman. Brahman is infinitely vast but spiritual in the sense of praying for the enlightenment of each Atman. The world looks material on the surface. But underneath the surface it is spiritual, nothing but Brahman in whom all things attain their enlightenment.

This view of the universe is interesting to us as we tremble with fear in the valley of nuclear annihilation. It urges us to realize in each atom and nuclear particle a part of Brahman such that atomic energy should be respected in terms of its metaphysical significance. It would be sacrilegious for mankind to use nuclear power for destructive purposes. Only for the purpose of advancing peace and realizing equality should it be used. Atoms are Atmans, which in turn are Brahman.

This Indian way of thinking is startling but suggestive. Today not only the West but also the East is apt to think in terms of division and conflict, without realizing the hidden interconnection of things at the deeper level. Too easily do we think of an opponent of ours as our enemy, while it is exactly this foe who can teach us something we should realize. So we deem Russia, China or Korea as our enemy. Thus we are surrounded by adversaries, while they can be the best teachers or stimulators we must have if we are to improve spiritually. The Hindu tradition, which is the mother of Zen, would stress interdependence of all things in the wide world. The so-called foe is our friend. A Japanese is an American. The Russian is a Britisher. In relation to the Absolute the difference between finite beings becomes almost nil. Modern mathematics deals with infinity∞, thus stating

$$\infty + 2,000 = \infty + 3,000.$$

Infinity is so incommensurably large that the difference between 2 and 3 dwindles into insignificance as soon as we put these two finite numbers side by side with infinity.[7] Thus Georg Cantor's finding seems to illustrate the validity of the Hindu insight into universal interwovenness.

Buddha gave a special meaning to the tradition of Zen. He made it more ethical through his moving experience. We should know something about this dramatic career of his.

The realm of Buddha's father's tribe was one of the smaller states in India in the fifth century before Christ. It was on the side of the Himalayan mountains in what is Nepal today. As Japan is sandwiched between the two mightiest nations of the world so this small state was situated between the strongest countries of India in those days, Kosala to the north-west and Magadha to the south-east. The little Sakya republic was actually ruled by the king of Kosala who received tribute from the former.[8] In the middle of the century the chief of this tribe was Suddhodana whose queen was Mahamaya, who gave birth to a divine son, Gautama, in 463 B. C. Gautama was a superior baby in every respect. But his mother died when he was seven days old and so mothered by her sister who became his father's queen. The child was superior physically, spiritually, intellectually. But he was unusual especially in his preference of quietness and meditation to the merry-makings and games characteristic of his age. When he was nineteen years old he was married to Yasodhara, an inspiring and intelligent girl of the same clan. No doubt their marriage was a joyous and blessed one.

But one day the young prince saw an old man; then a person with a disease; and then a dead body being carried to the cremation ground by sorrowful relatives. Lastly on the same day an ascetic walking with a determined manner along the highway. This made a deep impression on the prince, who had already been pondering over the ultimate fate of every living being. His mother had passed away. Many insects, lower animals and old people were dying. How about the future of a nation like his father's republic which was in a precarious, dangerous situation, between the two strongest kingdoms in all India? Perhaps this clearsighted prince foresaw something of the cruel fate of his father's castle which was destined to be captured when he was 72 years of age and all the people who were in that castle were to be massacred by the king of Kosala. At any rate, the prince had been determined to become a beggar priest; thus trying to solve the problem of death.

This is shown by the strange name Rahula, meaning "Obstacle", chosen for his first-born babe. The prince himself chose this ominous name for his son. He had already made up his mind to go away from his family. So this baby was another obstacle to the fulfilment of this secret wish of his. It was another tie of human endearment and affection, which would have to be broken if he was to forsake all his loved ones in his father's castle.

One night, after a sumptuous banquet held in the castle, he left home, casting his last glances at Yasodhara and the baby, who had been fast asleep. He tore himself away, and rode towards a forest, thus treading the road of meditation, away from all disturbances and distraction. There in the leafy arbor he tried to concentrate on the meaning of life, but the thought of his loved ones remaining in his father's castle, hunger and thirst, doubt and worry disturbed him so much that he decided to leave the forest. He visited three eminent teachers, one after another, finding all of them unconvincing. Gautama had thought more profoundly than they and his thirst for truth remained unquenched. So he left them, moving on, finally reaching a picturesque land, near modern Gaya, surrounded by wondrous woods through which ran a crystal-clear stream with banks of white sand. There in that lovely, quiet place, he practiced Zen.

Six years had passed since he left home. He had practiced the way of self-torture, which he found as fruitless as the way of pleasure he had tried in the palace, surrounded by singing and dancing girls. So here in this ideal school for meditation he was determined to stick to a third way of life, that was one of striking a happy medium between luxury and asceticism. Partaking of milk offered him by a native girl, taking a dip in the clear water of the River Niranjara, squatting on soft grass given him by a grass cutter, he meditated at the foot of a Bodhi tree. There he was enlightened when dawn was breaking on December the 8th, 428 B.C.

Early on the morning of December the 8th, 1941, the Pacific War began. Is it a mere coincidence that it began

on the same day when Gautama was enlightened, thus becoming the Enlightened One, Buddha? He must be mortified
because his finding was supposed to have nothing to do with
war. It was to show the best way to deal with the enemy,
restoring and maintaining peace, putting an end to the fear of
death itself. Gautama became Buddha on that day because
he discerned a newer, higher dimension in the meaning of
Zen, although the act of squatting and meditating was a
time-honored tradition in India. Buddha's personality, career,
intelligence, will to choose the golden mean, was unique.
And this made a difference to what he saw that morning. A
careful analysis of his epoch-making discovery is here in
order.

A Japanese Buddhist society enumerates some fifteen
thousand sutras which are worth studying if we are to understand the meaning of the content of Enlightenment on the
part of Buddha. And we are to cite some of the most convincing contentions of these sutras. We begin with early
Buddhism, for an account of which we have to depend on
the Pitakas, or the Basket of the Law. During the night before
December the 8th, 428 B.C., Gautama hit upon the fact of
universal causation, both temporal and spatial. All things
in the whole world, past, present and future, influence one
another profoundly. The main trouble with man is the fear
of death, which takes its rise due to selfishness and ignorance
of the fact of this causation. In the beginning there is this
ignorance, which causes all kinds of emotional disturbances,
including selfishness, narrowness, exclusiveness, irritation,
disappointment, worry, envy, enmity, will to do away with
one's opponent, will to power, frustration, the fear of all
disvalues, which center round the inevitable coming of destruction and death. The final outcome which is the fear of
death must be traced back ultimately to ignorance as to the
hidden interdependence of all elements of causation. Do away
with this ignorance, then the fear of death, together with all
the other disvalues and disturbances will disappear. This
ignorance is rooted in the narrowness of the selfish man. He

sees himself as a discrete being, independent of all other beings in the world, past, present, future.

Buddha deepened the traditional insight of India vastly in this sense. It used to be the realization of interwovenness of all entities only at the present moment, but he made it time-transcending. In other words he saw a new dimension in the time-honored idea of universal interdependence. What does it mean ethically? It means a deepening of the altruistic side of Indian thought. If interdependence is time-transcending, I am responsible for what will take place tomorrow or ten years hence. What I did in the past may be the cause of the misery, now impinging on someone in some far-off place. What I should have done but did not do last year might be making some one in another nation unhappy. The idea of corporate responsibility is thus made deeper and wider.

Summarizing the meaning of his own enlightenment, Buddha would say this. "I as a separate self do not exist. I am one of the minutest moments or chains of the law of universal causation. All other selves are just as dear to me as myself or my own son Rahula." He would continue to say that suppose one dies physically, that does not mean the death of all other selves which constitute a vast unity of the undying world process. One's influence is undying too. This way of viewing oneself and the world gives one the impression that his own soul has become as wide as the everlasting universe itself. All his petty disturbances disappear too. He now thinks of all men and all things as part of the wondrous unity, of which he himself is a minute constituent. Thus he stands reborn spiritually, with his loving hands lifted high to embrace all beings with undying compassion which is boundless and infinite. All the divisions and partitions which used to mar his spiritual purview disappear all of a sudden as if they were smoke. And he stands face to face with one global expanse of serene compassion. He is enlightened. Enlightenment is willy-nilly cosmic. Change which is individual or local is not worthy of being called enlightenment. Unlike a moralist who is apt to become conscious of his own superiority because he is a transformed

100

saint, the Buddha would refuse to be called enlightened unless all his fellows are equally enlightened.

> Enlightenment is real
> > Only when
> > > All are enlightened.

> Change is valid
> > Only when
> > > All are changed.

> No pride is sane
> > Unless and until
> > > All are transformed.[9]

The enlightened one is a new person who has obtained for the first time a vision of the Ultimate Reality which transcends all discriminations.

This vision was so marvellous even to Buddha himself that he was hesitant to begin to teach it to the people although he was certain that it would help them. But after a period of three weeks during which he enjoyed the aftermath of this discovery, he decided to pass this spiritual gem to the world which needed it. His teaching was fruitful to the superlative degree during forty-five years until he passed away at the age of eighty. His compassion warmed all hearts, healed many wounds, solved diverse problems. Whoever came under his influence became a new person, free from the affective disturbances which troubled him. A young man suffering from a rejected love, a criminal who used to take delight in murdering his fellow citizens, a young ruler who was sin-sick because he had usurped his own father's throne, were all transformed as they came to deal with him. He varied his message as he understood the special predicament in which each of these victims was, although the more profound principle which was at the root of each of his teachings was always the same vision of the Ultimate Reality and its Law of Universal Causation. The young man came to see that other young ladies could be

101

as good as the haughty girl who had rejected his love. The criminal saw that he had been killing his better self by murdering a fellow citizen. The sinful king realized that a genuine repentance and the decision to start a new life of compassion was the only way out of the situation he was in. Buddha would say this. "The moon which was hidden behind black clouds for a while would shine with a serener radiance when it comes out from behind them. So a repented criminal can be more markedly compassionate than someone who never sinned."[10]

Ultimately Buddha had no foe. His compassion rooted in the Cosmic Law transformed all those with whom he came into contact. What he once taught is applicable to his own evangelism and its effectiveness: "The fragrance of the tropical blossom, however rich it may be, does not travel against the wind. But the beneficent influence of a good man travels in all directions."[11] Confucius was a brilliant statesman but often he was up against those who tried successfully to get rid of him. But Buddha, though never a statesman, had the marvellous winsomeness and transforming radiance which converted even the most scheming enemy like his cousin, who wanted to succeed him prematurely and become the head of the preaching mendicants. But eventually he came under the benign influence. All this Buddha achieved through his quiet manners. "Muni"[12] which means "quiet saint" is what he was. His benign being was so full of compassion. He was so selflessly gracious that like the white bird, which flies faster and higher than the gay-clad peacock, he was most effective in bringing about good results. He was a genius in telling a vivid story. "A man should sometimes be like a snake which sloughs off its old skin, so that when anger arises within the heart, it and all the trace of this poisonous emotion should immediately be gotten rid of as if it were an old skin of the snake."[13] This teaching as to how anger should be removed from one's whole system quickly is found in the chapter on snakes, with which the most ancient Pali sutra of Buddhism, *Suttanipata* begins. Herein is an insight which both East and West must ponder over these days. Anger goes with pride. Vindictiveness is caused by it. Our judgment is befogged as soon as anger begins to take its rise within our system. Sometimes "righteous indignation" is spoken of as if it were a symbol of social justice. But I wonder whether this is wholly true. "Righteous indignation" is another name for impatience, haughtiness, superficiality.

Buddha warned people against slander too. When a baby is born it already has within its mouth a tiny hatchet. Whenever it speaks ill of anyone else the hatchet begins to cut the mouth from within itself. This is the way Buddha warned people against the harmfulness of slander.

All these insights and many others were obtained by him through his deep thought of the Ultimate Reality of Cosmic Causality. Pali sutras say that in the midst of his busy day he withdrew occasionally into a quiet place to practice Zen again. Thus he was able to tap cosmic law and resourcefulness by means of Zen practice. It reminds us of Jesus who occasionally withdrew into the mountain and prayed to God. It was his custom to have such a retreat, thus having a vital communion with God, receiving from him a moral support and personal guidance. This mountain top experienece was so vitally significant that we cannot understand him without understanding the superabundance of divine power he thus gained. So he taught his disciples to pray receptively and without ceasing. What prayer was to Jesus Zen was to Buddha.

Sometimes Jesus was friendless. Buddha taught his followers to go alone like the horn of the rhinoceros, which proceeds dauntlessly despite heat, rain, hunger, thirst.[14] What he meant by it is that a good man should mingle with all kinds of people everywhere, without disliking or discriminating against any one, but he should not be soiled with the greed, anger, and other affective disturbances of society, but continue to uphold the high moral standard of his own. Again Buddha would refer to a huge elephant which walked alone in the midst of a wintry forest.[15] Here too Buddha gives a symbol of noble independence in the midst of ethical mediocrity or corruption. It would be good to help and save all people. But one must be prepared to go alone sometimes. Sociability without solitariness is shallow.

Still the highest law of the universe is that of boundless, infinite compassion, without which no man can be blessed. Not that men are enlightened by being made the object of this compassion but that to be convinced of this law and practice it, is the only way to enlightenment. Here Buddha envisages all people of all ages because his own age, separated from other ages, is an infinitesimally tiny abstraction. This is the extent of the breadth of Buddhist compassion. It is said to be richer in content than Christian love because the former draws a bigger circle of compassion which takes in animals and inanimate things on which men are dependent for existence. Moreover, every object of compassion is viewed in terms of its past, present and future. There is still another difference between Christian love and Buddhist compassion, it seems to some. That is epistemological. The Hindu is epistemologically monistic in that the loving subject and the loved object are two members of the whole of the Ultimate Reality, so that both are inseparably interwoven with each other. On the other hand, the Christian thinks of a fellow as a separate, independent being. He sees a metaphysical gap between the two.

Some Christians ignore Paul's conviction that Christ lived in him. This is a monistic affirmation. Jesus too was convinced that his self-consciousness at its best was nothing but God-consciousness. God was in Christ in the true sense of the term. And God in Christ dwells in all men, who love God. Thus Christian epistemology is monistic, doing away with a naive dualism between the subject and the object. This realization does away with a falsely envisaged difference between love and Zen.

The testimony of sight agrees with common sense. But quantum theory says something like this. At the quantum level of precision,[16] the entire universe, including all observers of it, must be thought of as forming a single indivisible unit with every object linked to its surroundings by incompletely

104

controllable quanta. Quantum theory with its principle of complementarity, the uncertainty principle, the view of the wave-particle duality of matter, implies the validity of a view like the Hindu insight into the interwovenness of all things.

It is interesting to note that as modern mathematics advances and has come to be used by physics more and more, quantum theory seems to come closer and closer to the ancient view of the Hindu thinker. We realize also that the Bible is not devoid of some such insight because the seventeenth verse of the first chapter of Colossians affirms that in Christ all things hold together. There is another observation which coincides with the above. That is a realization on the part of clear-sighted observers of the specific feature of this atomic age to the effect that unless we all become cooperative members of one and the same world there will be no world at all.[17] Those of us who are appreciative of modern mathematics will realize also that although the world of mathematical ideas has become vastly multi-dimensional, each branch of it, exactly when it becomes generalized, dovetails[18] into another branch with an amazing coherence. It is marvellous that unusual assortment[19] of mathematical ideas found in various branches of this science has caused unexpected advance, as if to suggest that there is some more hidden unity beneath superficial divisions.

Buddha knew nothing about all this modern finding. But his cosmic intuition made him say something unforgettable: "A big stone is bound to sink and will never come up to the surface of the river, however ardently you may pray so that it may float on the face of the water. Just in a similar way all your prayer for enlightenment will be futile if you do not realize the root truth of the interwoven oneness of all men, all things and the rest of the universe."[20]

Buddha's thought was deep. But he knew how to make it easy when he was dealing with simple people. An illustration like the following was understood by serfs and day-workers. "Look at the stack of reeds before you. It stands because many stems are bound together near the top. You can never let only one reed stand on its end even when there is no wind. In a similar way we stand safely together when we realize our mutual interdependence. We are like a reed-stack."[21] His teaching was not didactic but pictorial. He made his hearers visualize the reed-stack in a peaceful country, thus inviting them to see the beauty of compassionate cooperation of their own accord. Buddha did not insist but inspire, and the hearers were convinced, consoled, converted into Buddha-like people. If the Veda is chiefly religious; the Upanishad philosophical; and the Buddhist sutra moral. The birds of the air, the moon travelling across the sky, the beauty and fragrance of blossoms, animals like snakes, rhinoceroses, elephants, snow-covered mountains, all other impressive phenomena in nature and life were used by Buddha as illustrations of the naturalness of compassion. He made infinite compassion as natural as the recurrence of the four seasons. He would point to a calm lake[22] in the mountains, convincing his people of the naturalness of the quiet and serenity of the compassionate soul, free from lower desires of complaint, greed, anger.

His hearers were enchanted, ecstatic, entirely ennobled. This is the experience of enlightenment. We understand Buddha saw a shining star[23] on the dawn of the morning of December 8th, 428 B.C., when he was enlightened. The star is still and yet speaks the eternal truth of the law of compassion which takes its rise as one understands the fact of interwovenness of all things in the world. Buddha's ethic is serene, still, and yet startlingly sound.

One thing he stressed is the sad fate of the vanquished. They lie down in shame and sorrow.[24] Victory breeds vindictiveness. He who is serene sleeps peacefully, away from victory and defeat. The ethic of the will to be free from victory is his. Often in the course of history goodness was too naively identified or associated with triumph. But one should never wish to be a victor. The only kind of victory which is good is the victory over one's own lower self. The enlightened one wills to make all others cross over to the land of bliss first, before he crosses over himself. He should be last to leave this world of pain. Let everyone else be a victor except himself: this is the motto of the Buddhist ethic. Victory engenders hatred and vindictiveness which cannot be done away with except by means of boundless compassion which is exactly the opposite of enmity. The vicious circle of victory and vindictiveness can be broken only through the ethic of tender care over the defeated. He who can be indifferent to victory is wise. He who can be taking a bird's-eye view of the panorama of history and realize that from a higher point of view victors down below are just as tragic as the defeated. Blessed are those who transcend all those swirls of triumph and defeat! They are the ones who comprehend profoundly the meaning of life. Beware of victory-hunters.

Now we are in the position to summarize what Zen meant to Buddha himself. He was a man of pain to begin with. He suffered deeply due to his own high intelligence, his responsibility to succeed his father in guiding the republic in the direction of safety and peace, more deeply because of his vicarious suffering for all those who have sorrow. He was enlightened as he saw that boundless compassion is the way of life. During those forty-five years of evangelistic work, he practiced Zen from time to time to make doubly sure that universal interwovenness of all things is the ultimate truth which is the natural mother of infinite compassion.

What did Zen mean for his followers? It meant for them to do as he did, following the Master's footsteps[25] in practicing the life of boundless compassion. The truth of universal interdependence of all things and values means for Buddhists to discern and appreciate whatever values which they do not represent themselves, for instance, the values of ethics and philosophies other than Zen Buddhism itself. This is why Zen is appreciative in the broadest sense of the term. Confucianism or Christianity is different from Zen. But Zen is appreciative of the unique values of either one of these. Zen knows no envy.

Zen in Japan

Once Japan was called
Yamato which means
Big benign peace

A new *Yamato* must
Come out of the ruins
Of a tragic war

From now on always
She should be
Truly *Yamato*

Have you ever tasted Japanese persimmon? It is the sweetest fruit in the world, provided you taste it when it is ripe. But when it is not quite ripe, it is astringent. It undergoes an amazing qualitative transformation in a short period of time. A man goes through a similar transformation through Zen. His raw human nature is "astringent", namely, self-centered, narrow, exclusive-minded, vindictive, angry. But the Zen-transformed man is sweet. He is boundless compassion itself. Zen is what Buddha himself practiced when he was enlightened and also from time to time during those forty-five years of his post-enlightenment life. This is original Zen in India. In China it was combined with Taoism, thus producing a more practical type of Zen. In Japan Zen has undergone a change in the sense of becoming a more radically self-transforming experience as in the case of a Japanese Zen master, Dogen, 1200-1253.[26] He thought of Zen as following Buddha, the Great Enlightener, and representing all values Buddhism has given birth to through the centuries, in India, China, and Japan. Dogen thus broadened the meaning of Zen immensely in regarding it as the General Headquarters of Buddhism. He also deepened its meaning by making the experience of self-transformation as thoroughgoing as Buddha himself had experienced it when he was first enlightened at the foot of the Bodhi tree.

Dr. Daisetsu Sazuki has written much about Zen. The West thinks of his interpretation of it as the only valid one. But some Japanese thinkers regard Dogen as one of the best Zen masters Japan has produced exactly in the sense that he tried to do what Buddha himself had done. The rigor with which the change of raw human nature into a Buddha-like soul is brought about is characteristic of Dogen's Zen. Further, his view of the world is unique in the sense of envisaging one Crimson Heart of Cosmic Compassion[27] taking the initiative of causing a man to wish to practice Zen so that he may be transformed. In viewing such a personal Enlightener in the cosmic context Dogen makes a contribution to the history of ethic, religion and philosophy. And yet his books have not been introduced to the Western reader as well as we might wish. Hence this attempt to explain Dogen's Zen here. Before we come to that, a brief review of the history of Buddhism in Japan is in order.

No one knows precisely when Buddhism came to Japan. It is not so visible as a vessel or vehicle. It is part of the air we breathe. It is part of the soul of a person and his experience. The year 552, however, is the recorded time when the Japanese people were supposed to have come into contact with Buddhism more officially, though its ideas must have come here before this date. Since then Japan has become one of the most Buddhistic nations in the world. Buddhism has flourished in Japan to a remarkable extent because some superior people of Japan have demonstrated its value through their own thought and deed. They have in turn added some uniquely Japanese characteristic to their Buddhism.

Prince Shotoku, 574-621, in the capacity of a member of the Imperial Household and an eminent statesman, did much in making the people appreciate the beauty of Buddhist compassion. He wrote a new splendid constitution[28] based on the spirit of equality which is an element of the infinite compassion of Buddha. Its fifth article teaches government officials to be especially understanding toward poor people, whose complaints should be listened to with unusual care. Its third article urges all the people to respect Buddhism as the ultimate guiding principle of men and the supreme religion for all nations, believing that it will bring about a universal peace and harmony among men and nations. Its tenth article warns against anger. Anger should be done away with under all circumstances and whenever two men disagree both of them may be wrong so that to be self-righteous is not only sinful but wrong. Its twelfth article teaches government officials never to exploit the masses of people and that the noble use of political power for the welfare of the masses should always be that at which the officials should aim. Its fifteenth article points out the presence of selfishness wherever grudges take their rise. Its last and seventeenth article is democratic in that all things should be discussed with people or their representatives.

Prince Shotoku's aspiration to purify politics by the spirit of boundless compassion is seen in the handsome statue of Buddha at Kamakura, which is based on a thousand petals of the lotus flower, adorning the foundation of this impressive statue. This symbolizes the ideal of having every part of this country under the benign jurisdiction of Buddha, since each of those lotus petals stands for each province of Japan.

> Among the foliage
> The Buddha statue
> Beautiful and benign

Those who have seen this image will long remember that an influential statesman like Prince Shotoku determined to devote his power to the compassion of Buddha so that men of prestige may always use their power for the whole people and not for the gratification of the desire of a few administrators. In this connection we should think about the contention of Eisai, 1141-1215, to the effect that as Zen flourishes the nation flourishes too.[29] He said that those rulers and cabinet members who abuse their power are devils and monsters. He implied that as Zen functions in statesmanship it will be like Jen which the three best emperors of ancient China practiced. Here the ideal of statesmanship is the primacy of the happiness of the people over the authority of the chief administrator, who takes the whole responsibility for the beneficent use of privileges.

Lowliness of heart is the second trait of Japanese Buddhism. This quality had been treasured by the people even before Buddhism came. The *haiku* shows it.

> The rice plant bows
> More and more lowly
> As it grows ripe

The rice plant comes to make a still more gracious bow as the dew of boundless compassion is on it. Buddha upholds the high ideal of enlightening all others before oneself, thus making a pure-hearted believer all the more lowly in spirit. Dengyo, 767-822, was the founder of Hiei Temple near Kyoto. He did such a great deal for helping and teaching and saving the people of Japan that he is respected by millions of people even today. Yet he once made a heartfelt confession to the effect that he is the most stupid among all the stupid and the most insane among all the insane.

> What is the sign of sanity?
> Not the sense of one's own goodness
> But that of one's own insanity
> Is the true proof of saintliness.[30]

The enlightenment of the slow and the stupid is the third earmark of Japanese Buddhism. This makes a contrast to Indian Buddhism, which stressed the enlightenment of bright minds like Kasyapa who alone smiled because he saw the meaning of Zen to be character-transformation occasioned by the death of the selfish self, when Buddha picked a flower in the presence of his best disciples; and to Chinese Zen, which emphasized the brilliance of men like Seccho Juken (Hsüeh-t'ou Chung-hsien, 980-1052) and Yengo Bukkwa (Yüan-wu Fokuo, 1062-1135), who compositely produced the

111

scholarly "Blue Rock Collection", namely, a treasury of Chinese Zen insights. Japanese Buddhists like Honen, 1133-1212, stressed the need of becoming like totally illiterate people because the learned were bound to be proud.[31] Honen claimed that the simplicity of Buddhist enlightenment is such as to be put on one small sheet of paper. The gist of it may be something like a perfect devotion to Amida, namely the Mahayana view of the Cosmic Personification of Boundless Compassion. According to Honen, the only way to enlightenment was the realization on one's part that all that he knows about Buddhism is a mere nothing and that the difference between him and a child is practically nil. This is striking when we see that Honen was a keen intellect, one of the most brilliant scholars of his days, and a most fascinating writer, poet, speaker.

Related to Honen's faith is the deep penitence[32] of Shinran, 1173-1262, Honen's prized disciple. Shinran examined his own life, desires, motivations, with utmost candidness, from the point of view of Amida's boundless compassion. Then he saw immediately how narrow, self-centered, wicked he was. He saw that whatever good he was able to think of or do was due to the initiative taken by Amida. He was wickedness itself, whereas Amida's goodness was infinitely rich. So Shinran ascribed all his disciples to Amida, saying, "I do not have a single disciple of my own."[33] This remark humbled those Buddhists round about him, who were disputing as to who was the most influential of them. Shinran's self-criticism was growing severer and severer as he grew older. And yet when he realized how good Amida had been to him all those years, he thought he should be infinitely grateful to Amida and do good out of the sense of profound gratitude. "I have not done anything good of my own accord and yet Amida has bestowed upon me so much compassion. So, not out of the sense of obligation, but out of the deep sense of unspeakable thankfulness, I must rededicate myself to the task of saving the masses of people."[34] So thinking, Shinran continued to preach on the blessed news of enlightenment by faith alone. His thought is the theme of this song of mine.

> All the ill is due to me.
> No good I can do nor think.
> Amida takes the initiative,
> Does all the good in life,
> Saves all souls in the world.
>
> Thanksgiving, deep, sincere, heartfelt,
> Is what I feel deep down.
> Out of this sense of gratitude
> For Amida's infinite compassion
> I cannot help but do good.

Persecution has a religious meaning.[35] This is what Nichiren, 1222-1282, testified to the East through his own experience, just as Jesus blessed the persecuted in the Western hemisphere. Nichiren was a fisherman's son who was inspired into becoming a prophet and a savior in time of unprecedented national crisis. He was persecuted, exiled, beaten, had his left arm broken, was about to be killed more than once, because he had declared his own Buddhism as the only good kind. This claim was due to the fact that he regarded the Lotus Sutra, to which he was devoted, as the most authoritative of all Buddhist Sutras. He argued that the persecution he was undergoing was the fulfillment of the prophecy recorded in the Lotus Sutra, which was the most realistic description of the hardship which Buddha had endured. So realizing Nichiren could not only endure his own hardship but also glory in the mission he was privileged to fulfill. Buddha in hardship was the symbol of Nichiren's own fate and also Japan's, when the Mongolian invasion was imminent. So Nichiren said to all Japan that she should devote herself to the Sacred Lotus Sutra which would be sure to rescue the whole nation. Nichiren was right. The mighty navy of the Mongolians was annihilated by a terrific storm off the coast of the Island of Kyushu before it arrived in Japan.

Nichiren continues to inspire people who are in hardship for the sake of their religious conviction. Today in Japan there is a Buddhist sect called Soka Gakkukai. This sect is politically influential, reflecting the vigor and aggressiveness derived from Nichiren's devotion to the Lotus Sutra.

The meaning of the Buddhist prayer was deepened by men like Yukan, 1649-1716. He testified through his own life that prayer is valid only when it is intercessory.[36] The nature of Buddhist compassion is such that it prays for the enlightenment of all others, prior to that of one who prays. To pray for oneself is against the truth of this compassion. Moreover, prayer should be ardent as if the present prayer were the very last prayer one can ever offer in all his life. "Say each prayer as if it were the last prayer on the deathbed." This is the burden of the sermon Ippen, 1268-1325, preached repeatedly.[37] Here the implication is that the only moment at which one can be sure to be able to do good at all is the present moment, the unique values of which should, therefore, be appreciated to the fullest extent. Religion is not merely otherworldly but this-worldly in this sense. So one should not postpone until another time what he is able to do here and now.

Japanese Buddhism is like an impressive range of summer clouds. Each indentation of columns of this cloud formation is lovely against the background of deep blue. One of them is particularly splendid. That is Dogen's Zen. He said that the whole range, not one or two of these indentations, is good. Zen is the sum of all values of Buddhism, Indian, Chinese, Japanese. Dogen stressed the need of becoming a new, wholly-altruistic self through Zen, because he wanted to follow Buddha whose enlightenment meant to become a boundlessly compassionate saint, free from self-centered feelings. The Zen transformation which Dogen experienced is to be the beginning of social, cosmic enlightenment. One man like Buddha becomes truly compassionate, thus causing others to be likewise. This causation is to become world-wide until the whole cosmos will eventually be transformed. Here Dogen refers to the work of the Crimson Heart of Cosmic Compassion in the universe. This ultimate reality is the cause of every kind of self-ennoblement on the part of each entity. Here the difference between men and atoms is not absolute because men depend for their existence upon the world of atoms. The difference between Zen and deed is not absolute. Zen deepens one's mercy. Compassionate deed is Zen in action. Deed, word, vow are all expressions of Zen, which in turn is the fruit of the ceaseless activity of the cosmic compassion. Here the Upanishadic view of the atom interpreted in terms of the spiritual unit of the universe is restored. The atom is Atman to be thought of as its potential union with God the Brahman. Dogen stands for this view. That is why we of this atomic age should listen to him for a hint as to the peaceful use of nuclear power, the possible misuse of which makes the future of man's destiny so gloomy these days. Learning from Dogen we should realize the divine destiny of each atomic nucleus. There in this minutest kernel is hidden the mightiest force to be used for the peace of God. But too many people miss this truth. The monadology of Leibniz or the world of occasions White-head framed comes close to Dogen's view of the universe of men and Atmans, rooted in the Crimson Heart of Cosmic Compassion. Dogen knows no science, thus remaining on a low level in comparison with Leibniz or Whitehead. But Dogen is most vivid in stressing the universal functioning of the Cosmic Compassion even in the minutest dimension. He would say that even dust shines with compassion in the sight of the enlightened.

Truth does not necessarily depend on modernity alone. Atoms must be seen from the point of view of peace-making and love-practicing. God works in atoms too. No sacrilege should be permitted.

REFERENCES

Chapter III

1. S. Radhakrishnan, **Indian Philosophy**, Volume I, p. 21, Chapter II; vol. II, p. 772, George Allen & Unwin, London, 1923. H. Nakamura, **The History of Indian Thought**, chaps. I, V, IX, X. Iwanami Shoten, Tokyo, 1956.
2. Samādhi is a Pali word, which means concentration. This is to bring peace of mind and stability of morale. **Suttanipata**, verse 226, or the oldest collection of Buddha's sermons, translated by H. Nakamura, **Buddha no Kotoba**, Iwanami Shoten, 1958.
3. Dhyāna is a Pali word, the euphonic transcription of which is Zen. **Indian Philosophy**, vol. I, p. 424-7.
4. **Indian Philosophy**, vol I, 22.
5. **Ibid.**, Chap. II.
6. **The History of Indian Thought**, p. 24, 269.
7. I. P. Natanson, **Theory of Functions of a Real Variable**, p. 89 Frederick Ungar Publishing Co., 1955.
8. **2500 Years of Buddhism**, edited by P. V. Bapat, p. 20, Government of India, The Publications Division, Delhi, 1959.
9. My poem.
10. F. Masutani, **Kyoten no Kotoba**, "Words of Sutras", p. 113, Shudosha, Tokyo, 1957.
11. **Ibid.**, p. 130.
12. "Muni" means a saint devoted to the enlightenment of all men through holy quietness. **Suttanipata**, verse 207.
13. **Suttanipata**, verse 3.
14. **Ibid.**, verse 52.
15. **Buddhist Sutras**, edited by Tokyo University, p. 98, Sansheido, Tokyo, 1955.
16. D. Bohm, **Quantum Theory**, p. 584, Prentice-Hall, 1951.
17. **Nuclear Weapons and the Conflict of Conscience**, edited by J. C. Bennett, p. 120, Scribners, 1962.
18. A. N. Whitehead, **An Introduction to Mathematics**, p. 71, 84, Oxford Univ. Press, London, 1919 (1953).
19. **Ibid.**, 101.
20. "Words of Sutras", p. 168.
21. **Ibid.**, p. 9.
22. **Suttanipata**, verse 467.

23. This reminds me of Kant who aspired to be more sublime as he stood below the star-dotted sky.
24. "Words of Sutras", p. 69.
25. Dogen, **Shobogenzo**, "True Dharma Nuclear Treasury", edited by Sokuo Eto, vol. I, p. 56, Iwanami Shoten, Tokyo, 1949.
26. H. Ui, **General Treatise on Buddhism**, vol. II, p. 473, Iwanami Shoten, 1948.
27. "True Dharma Nuclear Treasury", vol. III, p. 11.
28. **Buddhist Sutras**, p. 365.
29. **Ibid.**, p. 485.
30. My poem. **Buddhist Sutras**, p. 376.
31. **Buddhist Sutras**, p. 452.
32. **Ibid.**, 587.
33. **Ibid.**, p. 596.
34. **Ibid.**, p. 587.
35. N. Iino, **Christ and Buddha**, p. 108, 131, Risosha, Tokyo, 1957.
36. **Buddhist Sutras**, p. 663.
37. **Ibid.**, p. 627.

Preface to Chapter IV

The World Diagnosed

Two husky giants
    On a long see-saw
        Balanced over an abyss

Like Don Quixote
    They really mean well
        But are both youthful

The world looking on
    Is scared stiff
        While Castro dances wildly

The global fear
    Of escalation, megadeath
        And total destruction

The horrible arms race
    Must be checked
        Somehow, somewhere, shortly

There is no one panacea
    Under the grace of God
        All things good count

Provincialism

Beware of three traits:
    Provincialism, also,
        Prejudice, pride

Provincialism in time
   And in space
      Breeds prejudice

Prejudice has
   Its oldest roots
      In dogmas of religion

Dogmas naively believed
   Engender pride,
      The breeder of all evil

Hence the dire need
   Of a long look,
      Self-scrutiny, prayer

Cooperation

Let us have three traits:
   Conviction, indeed,
      Contrition, cooperation

Conviction arises
   Through a synoptic view
      Of civilized history

Contrition must purge
   Our conviction lest
      We become complacent

A good combination
   Of these two alone
      Can bring cooperation

Continuously collecting
   And connecting
      All data of experience

Avoiding the conspiracy
Of selfishness
And narrow nationalism

Change is good
Only when all men
And all places change

The Ocean Liner
To Cross the Sea of Death

God prepares for man
An Ocean Liner
Equipped to cross
The Sea of Death

It is made of values
Which are immortal
In their objectivity
Rooted in God's will

It is made of atoms
Which are his body
God himself steers
This mammoth steamer

Those who are blind
With hatred, anger,
Past grievances, revenge
Are unable to see this ship

But those who love all
Pray for mankind
In all its entirety
Can take this divine ship

Her voyage will begin
Guided by God himself
Who is trustworthy
Beyond the fear of overkill

Nations are transient
But men dedicated
To God, Love, and Truth
Are surely immortal

God, the cosmic concreter,
Has shown his will
In love which promises
The highest fulfilment of man

Death is the beginning
Of a more spiritual life
More snugly attuned
To the cosmic concreter

Fear not. Just devote
Yourself to God's ideals,
Love, Equality, Freedom
In your eternal pilgrimage

Where are Nineveh, Babylonia?
Proud nations are dead.
But Christ crucified and
His martyred disciples live on.

Tyrants and dictators
Are as ephemeral
As dews in the morning.
The cosmic concreter abides.

The growing togetherness
Of all beings, Space, Time
Is achieved by the will
Of the cosmic concreter.

We who are peace-makers
Are truly invulnerable,
Against all weapons
Nuclear and absolute.

We live, move, and abide
In this holy receptacle
Beyond the change and decay
Of all entities in this cosmos.

Love and Peace

To conduct nuclear tests is hard
But to be a joyous self is easy.
Let us be changed beings,
Thus finding out what we are.

I cannot fully guarantee
Whether or not I am right.
I'd rather err, be on His side
By upholding the cause of peace.

Through the centuries
Men have always fought
In the name of justice
Which is pride in disguise.

For the first time in history
We have come to see today:
Self-preservation is the same
As pure love, undiscourageable.

If you uphold non-pacifism
You make yourself warlike.
Your principle is bound to mould
Your inner being in due time.

Men rely on power as long as
They are powerful and strong.
Problems solved by power
Will breed seeds of revenge.

Only love is able to solve
All problems in an ultimate sense.
Furthermore, love enables us
To find the true destiny of ours.

Until I came to live in America
Where prejudice against me was dense
I had not seen the love of God
Working in men's hearts and history.

It is through utter solitariness
And realization of one's frailty
That he comes to see vividly
The transforming nature of love.

You students from overseas:
You in this land have chance
To rethink the value of love,
Jen, Zen and moral influence.

Let us be peace-makers,
Tension-easers, schism-bridgers,
Whole-makers, framers of
A history, new and peaceful at last.

Ethic is an art. It is poetry,
The art of loving, including mankind
In our loving hearts, attuned
To God who embraces all with love.

Ah, ICU

Upon the Christian fellowship
    Of various races
        And many cultures
            May abundant blessings always dwell.

The heavenly felicity
　　Of practicing sacrificial
　　And forgiving mercy
　　　　Under the banner of our God.

The greatest privilege
　　Of producing makers
　　　　Of a new, peaceful history
　　　　Is our aspiration always.

Ah, ICU,
　　Fruit of prayer
　　In all Christendom.

Ah, ICU,
　　Hope of the world.
　　　　The Glory of its steady, sure advance.

Ten Years

Endless recollections this woodland invokes.
Our ten years: one expanse of bliss.
Prayerfully following eternal Christ
We work and worship in his name.
Gathering from all over the world,
Building here this house of study:
The founders of ICU have achieved
Something epoch-making through his grace.

Prayer

A small Japanese girl in Shizuoka Prefecture wishes to die, embracing her mother when total war ever begins. An American youth dreams the dream of mutual annihilation of the United States and the Soviet Union, because the world tension is growing truly marked in the fall of 1962.

Since the 22nd of October the Cuba incident had been shaking the world. Kennedy, Khrushchev, Castro, U Thant, Russell, Reynolds were spotlighted those days. Which one of these famous men stood for love? Who stood for power? Can love be combined with power? How about justice which is said to be a happy combination of love and power?

Power is needed by politics. But it does two things. It functions under the banner of justice, thus working toward self-preservation. So far so good. Here begins, however, a strange transformation. Justice begins to be changed into selfishness which in turn engenders aggressiveness.

> Throughout the ages
> Men have always fought
> In the name of justice
> Which is pride in disguise.

This atomic age is ominous with the danger of escalation. No nation is strong enough. Even a small nation could destroy a large one if the former strikes out first. No nation could win, scoring a shining victory. Power, which alone can bring about justice, may also bring a total holocaust of the world. Even when power is effective it might bring new problems hard to solve.

Love does two things. It can bring the highest self-fulfilment of a person by relating him to all values of the cosmos. Love establishes golden bridges between the self and all other realities of the world, thus filling it with the richness of all values. But it is so pure and defenseless that it may be destroyed by a loveless power set to extend its realm of safety and self-preservation. Christ could not save himself, though he is the most fruitful savior of all men in all ages. So statesmen never take love seriously while moralists aspire to adhere to love at any cost. And an attempt to strike a happy medium between the two is more or less an unstable equilibrium. Love gives all to others whereas power gains all for itself. Strength is intensified by meanness or lack of love,

125

whereas love is most genuine when it is devoid of any wish to think about its own self-preservation.

Jen and Zen are tender nieces of Christian love. They are one in the sense of taking the point of view of the whole of mankind. Jen stresses responsibility; Zen indivisibility; Love sacrifice. Because they are thoroughly whole-seeing they wholly go beyond the point of view of the ego-centricism of the individual. These three ideals are three views of Ultimate Reality from which all men and things come. Finite men and things come and go. But Ultimate Reality remains for ever. It is eternal, immortal, infinite. All ethics, all religions and all philosophies culminate in the view of Ultimate Reality, which alone is able to solve all problems, including the tension between love and power. Love, Jen, Zen gain some unshakable rootage and immeasurable cogency when they are viewed in their relation to this Rock of Ages, God, Heaven, Tao. Peace never comes until all men, Kennedy, Khrushchev, U Thant, Castro, Russell, Reynolds, humble themselves before the ancient altar of Ultimate Reality. As Kipling put it:

> "The tumult and the shouting dies,
> The captains and the kings depart,
> Still stands thine ancient sacrifice:
> An humble and a contrite heart."

The global transformation of proud souls is needed until love, Jen, Zen supplant the cut-throat competition of power-obsessed men and nations, saying, "God alone is strong enough." Divine love is another name for the poise of Tao, the sacrifice of Christ, the compassion of Zen, the peace of cosmic tranquillity.

> The Seer prays:
> Drop from above
> Heavenly stillness,

126

            And peace which
                Passes all strife,
                Human prowess,

            Patience, hope,
                Faith and bliss,
                Perspective.

Success is only in Heaven. What comes out of man returns to
man. Heaven gives unsparingly what men cannot achieve.
Once again we renew our devotion to Christ who taught us to
pray, not my will but thine be done. Not our desire to gain
power but his adherence to patience, forgiveness, love is the
way to peace.

The puzzle about love and power should not trouble us
too much. Even the most precise of all sciences, namely,
mathematics is not clear as yet as to what is true mathe-
matically. Mathematics is admitted to be a science in its
infancy. Quantum theory is based on the principle of inde-
terminacy. Ethic needs to be humble, without claiming too
much for its contention.

            Two young giants
                On a see-saw
                Balanced over an abyss

            They have been
                Moving more widely
                Apart from each other

            This nuclear age
                With the fear of
                Hot escalation . . .

            Still God reigns
                That they may change
                Their inner resolve

Ah, the greatness
   Of his concern
      About both giants

Mankind is one.
   Peace, love, Jen
      Zen, Tao are divine

Crisis is chance
   For all to see
      God is our refuge

Frozen stereotypes,
   Thought habits in
      Nations, big and small

Can be ennobled
   Through a synoptic
      View of history

This ennoblement,
   If realized,
      Will bring about peace

So speaks God
   Through consciences
      Purged by prayer

What remains unsaid
   Is the most important
      In any critical time

What remains unsaid
   Is God himself
      And his high ideals

Be still and know
   That nations are
      Transient like dews

But human souls
  Are truly immortal
    In the bosom of God

Once Japan relied
  On military strength
    Which ruined her

America and Russia
  Are asked to review
    The history of nations

Relying on strength
  All old empires
    Ruined themselves

Strong nations undefeated
  In modern war
    Still rely on strength

For them strength is
  The savior absolute
    And love is vain

Beware of this false Savior
  Who has betrayed once
    Tyre, Egypt, Babylonia

God is the true Lord
  Of history and the world
    Where strength defeats itself

This is the voice
  Of a nation first washed
    With atomic catastrophe

You strong giants,
  Both of you are asked
    To listen to this voice

129

It is not too late
For you can come
To a peaceful agreement

Forgive and understand,
Think of the future
Which can either be

A black holocaust
Of all things
And all nations

Or a bright bliss
Of peace and love
Prevailing in the world

P. Chandrasekhara Rao, a member of the Indian Society of International Law has contributed an article entitled, "The Non-Nuclear Powers and Disarmament" to the Weekly Supplement of the Japan Times, November 4, 1962. In it he holds what we all would like to agree to, that the non-aligned nations realize that they have lately acquired an inflated importance in the task of maintaining peace in the world. The advantage of a non-aligned nation lies in its ability to view the tension between the two power blocs from a neutral angle, which comes closer to the point of view of all mankind. Japan is so closely aligned with America that we are apt to believe what America believes. We should be unusually patient in trying to gain an objective view of the present situation in which Russia is not what she used to be under Lenin, Trotzky or even Stalin. Under Lenin and Trotzky the Soviet Union aimed at conquering the capitalistic world for Communism. But their secular-messianic hope was not fulfilled.

The failure of this hope and the ensuing victory of Stalin brought about a change in the nature of Soviet Communism. The death of the old Bolsheviks meant that of the old revolutionary idea. Stalin's slogan of "socialism in one country" meant the rapid industrialization of Russia. The Stalinist system was not a revolutionary system but a statism based on economic centralization.

Khrushchevism means reduction of political terror, capital accumulation, enough consumption. Yet it is a conservative, class-ridden regime, humanly coercive and economically effective. This is the exact opposite of true socialism. Despite these facts the Russians try to convince frustrated folk in Asia that Khrushchevism stands for socialism and a classless society. Within the Soviet Union Communist ideology has worn thin. Those who take this ideology seriously are the people of western nations.

What is clear to neutral nations and unclear to American-aligned nations is the tension between Russia and China. This tension is caused by two reasons. First, China under the older idea of Communist revolutionism, desires to extend its power. Second, Chinese leaders are not so sane as Russian leaders. Whether or not political leaders are sane is not a matter of accident. Any government which tries to do the economically impossible is apt to create fanatical leaders like the Chinese leaders who talk about justice when many Chinese people are poverty-stricken, whereas the Russian leaders today are realistic men of common sense because the Soviet Union is now able to solve its economic problems independently.

Japan is an American-aligned nation. The best thing American-aligned nations can do is to be calm. America is the strongest nation of the world in this sense. She has inherited from the Pilgrim forefathers the rare Christian resources of patience, divine perspective, love which would include even the enemy. These Christian insights are able to cope with all problems, personal, social, international. God is the God of all mankind. This is an eternal truth which can serve to support all men in this era of global fear and frustration.

I had the privilege of studying in America for ten years when Japan was a militaristic nation. My American teachers and friends convinced me about the Christian resources of the unity of all men, divine perspective, long-suffering, love that would draw a circle of undiscourageable mercy, taking in even the most staunch enemies.

Today, twenty years afterwards, I have the privilege of teaching American students at ICU, something about ways to peace. If my observation of these fine American youths is not mistaken they give me this impression. Their fatherland, America, is tempted to go the way of preparedness just as Japan was in 1941. Then I was a pacifist, thus enduring the pain and humiliation of being beaten, knocked down, kicked by soldiers of the Imperial Army.

So this is my sincere prayer.

> God of all mankind
>> Thou art strong enough,
>>> Thou alone, no others.
>
> May Thou bless America
>> Most abundantly
>>> At this time of crisis.
>
> Thou art the source
>> Of all values
>>> Sublime and serene.
>
> Peace is Thine aim
>> In the drama of
>>> Cosmic redemption.
>
> It will surely come
>> As men become still
>>> And know Thy will.
>
> We beseech Thee today
>> That Thou wouldst show
>>> The signs of the times
>
> To all mankind
>> Especially to America,
>>> The hope of the world.
>
>>>> Amen.

Graduation Service, March 17, 1963

Lord, thou art so merciful as to guide us to worship thee in this sanctuary rich in treasured memories of fellowship and consecration, blessedness and rebirth. Thou once guidedst our forefathers by the still small voice amidst thunder and earthquakes. We are grateful to thee for the rich guidance of thine through the ministry, parable, resurrection, of Jesus Christ our master.

At this graduation service we pray sincerely for these young leaders of the future world, who are about to commence their post-graduation work of Christian service and truth-finding, more advanced and complex. Continue to sustain them that they may be champions of peace, grace and noble adventure. Make them see here and now that they still have within themselves titanic possibilities of growth, waiting to be realized like seeds which have never been blessed by sunshine and rain, and that their true self-fulfilment will depend upon the extent to which they will rededicate themselves to thee. Enable them to become framers of a nobler history worthy to be called the forerunner of the Kingdom of Heaven.

Bless friends of ICU everywhere in the world. Inspire and reinforce the administration of this school, and all those whose prayer and cooperation make it possible for ICU to function with conviction and courage, gladness and gratitude, effectiveness filled with the heavenly sublimity of thine own truth.

We are grateful to thee for the conviction that nothing can separate us from thy radiant identity, in which we live, move, have our comfort. Our physical separation is another occasion on which we entrust our friends to thee. Fill us with the hope of an eternal pilgrimage under the guidance of immortal Christ whom we follow every passing moment in the spirit of prayer. In his name, Amen.

Chapter IV

HAIKU: Composed at Coe, BU, SUI

Three-hued

The heart of *Haiku*
　　Has three hues
　　　　Subdued, sincere, strong

As Mt. Fuji is hidden
　　Behind the Spring haze
　　　　So is *Haiku* subdued

As cherry blossoms
　　Are spotlessly pink
　　　　So is *Haiku* sincere

As the carp darts
　　Through the clear torrent
　　　　So is *Haiku* strong

Subdued, sincere, strong
　　It is a self-expression
　　　　Enduring, ennobled, ecstatic

Haiku in Japanese

Why is Haiku possible?
　　The reasons for this
　　　　Are three in number

The Japanese language
　　Is poetic, polite, pensive
　　　　This is the first reason

The Japanese sentiment
　　Is subdued, suggestive, strong
　　　This is the second reason

The Japanese tradition
　　Is rare, rich, ramified
　　　This is the third reason

The faint flavor of *Haiku*
　　Is somehow put across
　　　Even when it is written in English

This flavor will ennoble
　　The language, sentiment
　　　And tradition of another people

Haiku can be a bridge
　　Spanning East and West
　　　Two races, pragmatic and poetic

Complete Coherence

There is only one cosmos
　　Where complete coherence reigns
　　　Away from conflicts of cultures

That is the cosmos of mathematics
　　Where dreams come true perfectly
　　　When we have insights to see congruence

Actual life is a perpetual compromise
　　Between the ideal and the real
　　　A long second-best it remains to be

Ah, let us revisit the thought world
　　Where perfection is seen iridescent
　　　At every turn, in every dimension

This citadel of coherence
  Revisited from time to time
    Gives one the courage to live on

Three Months at Coe

Three blessed months
  I have spent at Coe College
    In Cedar Rapids, Iowa

Each passing moment
  Of the period thrills me
    With new values rare

The *Haiku* ditties contained
  In this lovely booklet
    Are gems of gratitude

Like the sun-lit dews
  On the "morning-glory"
    These *Haiku* scintillate

With the glitter and glow
  Of the grace of God
    Who is the source of good

He is guiding us always
  As our Coe friends bestow
    Precious, purple gifts on Noriko and me

So between classes, before retiring
  I have jotted down spontaneously
    Three hundred *Haiku* contained here

My Song

The song I would sing
  Is a dear old ditty
    Hummed softly, modestly

136

Others may not hear
   This singing to please
      The inmost core of my being

But if you would join me
   In this heartfelt singing
      You will be one with me in spirit

The Simple Charm

The beauty of the Chinese poem (*with 28 characters*)
   Which was composed by Li Po
      Has dignity and rhythm

It soars like noon-day clouds
   Floating like dreams
      Noble, shining, thrilling

The Japanese *Waka* (*31 syllabled*) we compose
   Do not have such a thrill
      Although it is simple, heartfelt

It clings to the ground
   Like the green moss
      Or the purple violet tiny

Yet there is a special sense
   In which it is unforgettable
      With the pulse-beat of the earth

Haiku (*17 syllabled*) is still simpler
   Both in form and content
      Akin to a dew-drop on the grass

This tiniest gem of the earth
   Mirrors the charm of life
      And the myriad-hued cosmos

Learning Zen at Coe

One thing I disliked
When I was a child
Was writing an essay

One thing I dreaded
When I was a lad
Was making a speech

One thing I abhorred
When I was a boy
Was cooking a meal

Since I came to Coe
I have cultivated
A taste for cooking meals

Writing, speaking, cooking
Are now hearty enjoyments
Thanks to my Coe assignment

To see rare values
Hitherto concealed to one
Is the meaning of Zen

Coe has taught me
A greater application
Of Zen teaching to life

Confucius

Once Confucius deplored
No student of his loved
Learning as much as romance

I have been really fortunate
In having eighty students
In my *Zeal for Zen* class

138

I am most delighted
  To meet you, Lucile,
    Because you love to study

The noblest kind of friendship
  Is rooted in a common zeal
    For truth-seeking disinterested

May we stimulate each other
  Teach, inspire, console . . .
    From now on, for years to come

A Ph.D. in Cooking

When my guests eat
  What I have cooked
    They say it tastes good

Whey my friends hear
  Me sing Japanese songs
    They say they like them

When they read my poems
  They spontaneously say
    That they respond to them

I am a Ph.D. in ethics,
  Not in cooking, singing,
    The composition of poems

But cooking and singing,
  Also writing ditties in English
    Are all part of my ethics

Exactly Here

Exactly in the commonest
  Life-situation here and now
    Is the most profound truth

The best, noblest folk
  We find if and only if
    Our eyes of appreciation are opened

To see them in their growth
  In the future years to come
    Through our eyes of ardent prayer

Forgetting their past mistakes
  Consistently trusting in them
    In terms of their moral maturity

This is the only way
  To our own blessedness
    A great fruit, unexpectedly won

Happiness always is
  A surprising by-product
    Obtained through love of others

Japan

Her sight, sound, scent . . .
  Chrysanthemums, white breakers
    The tonic fragrance of the sea.

Mt. Fuji is snow-clad
  Towering over the green lee
    Dotted with pink cherry blossoms.

The bamboo groves green
  The rice-fields golden
    Steeped in the sunbeams bright.

Tokyo is the biggest city
  With eleven million people
    Living in a super-modern capital.

The Japanese inn hospitable
　　Going the second mile of grace
　　　Making westerners feel ecstatic.

The fried shrimp, sukiyaki,
　　The rice wine warmed, raw fish,
　　　Waiting for you from America.

The geisha girls these days
　　Will greet you in American English
　　　Shaking hands with you all.

Self-belittlement

Exactly a gifted man or woman
　　Suffers from a lack of self-confidence
　　　As excellence and ecstasy flicker.

Exactly the best student here
　　Suffers from the sense of self-belittlement
　　　Hence the need of my constant prayer.

"When in disgrace with men's eyes and fortune
　　I all alone beweep my outcast state"
　　　So said Shakespeare at one time.

Jeremiah, William James, many men of genius
　　Keep company with you when you too suffer
　　　In the same way in which genius suffers.

So my ardent appeal to you all
　　Is just this: You must believe in yourselves
　　　Because you have in you inherent greatness.

Like seeds which have never been watered
　　And so have never grown, you are
　　　Wires which will shine incandescent with ideals.

141

Ideals of patience, devotion, diligence
   Forgiveness, compassion, and peace
      Will be the halo adorning you.

Be of good cheer, see through exteriors
   Into shining possibilities of
      Future growth and representative capacity.

Haiku

A spontaneous self-expression
   Brings about a joy unspeakable:
      So *haiku* is a delight.

It is like a scented flower
   Serving as a good guide
      For the butterfly's travel.

Haiku is not only a joy
   But a guide for men
      Who find in it life's mile-stone.

There lies curled in this bloom
   A faith boundless, rich
      In the promises of a good fruit.

The joy, good, and faith
   All bespeak for you
      The coming of a brighter day.

The Setting Sun

Japan used to be
   The land of the sun
      Rising with splendor.

Today she shivers
   In the valley of
      Fear and pain.

142

The land of the setting sun
Prays for peace
Amid strong powers.

Her hope is in hard work,
Prayer to God who
Sustains all history.

The defeated weep
In shame
And agony.

The mental sky
Is all dark
And stormy.

The rainbow
Of Zen insight
Suddenly appears

Illumining
All the world
Zenith, horizon.

Wonder

Often I marvel
At this truth:
All good things are hard.

Thus truth is
Beyond the reach
Of mediocrity.

God is eager
To teach us all
Love of patience.

143

Congratulations

Congratulations, Lucile,
  You are working on
    Your Ph.D. in America.

In a Japanese university
  It is not exactly academic
    But more honorary in fact.

"Apple polishing" of a kind
  With your major professor
    Would be really necessary.

All this unpleasant
  Forced apprenticeship
    You are free from here.

Japan's Charm

One big chrysanthemum
  White, fragrant, twelve-petaled:
    This is Japan at her noblest.

Wherever you may be
  The scent of the sea braces you:
    This is Japan at her finest.

The hue of the blue sky
  Is more soothing than indigo:
    This is Japan at her best.

The rice-field is green in summer
  Richly golden in autumn:
    This is Japan at her holiest.

Various values of modernity
  Melt with ancient tradition:
    This is Japan's fascination.

144

My Class

The first snow-fall
  Has muffled the noise of traffic
    Perfect stillness makes music all night.

The tinkling symphony
  Of the quiet atmosphere
    Thrills me profoundly.

Here in Cedar Rapids
  We eighty truth-seekers
    Blessed to contemplate

On the meaning of life,
  Death, peace, truth, bliss:
    Values of civilization too.

Rich in friendships
  American, Jewish, Chinese
    We pray very gratefully.

May our young friends
  Be blessed abundantly
    And all the time to come.

May we all fulfill
  Our powerful potentialities
    Under the heavenly grace.

Mutual Appreciation

I was interviewed on TV
  By an American lady
    Who had a kimono on

I had an American suit on
  While she asked me
    Interesting questions

Which is Japanese
    Which is American
        Mutual appreciation indeed

Once in a while
    Japan should put herself
        In the position of America

Once in a while
    America should put herself
        In the position of Japan

On the Question of Sex a Jewish Lad Asked Me

One quiet afternoon
    A ceremonial tea service
        Was conducted by a Zen man.

By mistake he dropped,
    Broke into two pieces
        The ceramic tea-container.

But then and there
    He glued them together
        With a divine dexterity.

Unexpectedly this heightened
    The worth of this caddy
        Now changed into a nobler form.

Like a ceramic caddy
    Dropped, broken, patched up
        Our value is sin-enhanced.

We are blunder-ennobled
    Our mistakes teach us
        Meekness, modesty, compassion.

146

We are like snow, sympathetic
    Veiling all blemishes kindly
        Making ugly scars white.

Our past blunders
    Have made us humble
        Through the healing grace of God.

Every disvalue should be
    A precious occasion on which
        God transforms our frailty.

The truly loving glance
    Is one which covers up
        Praying ardently when sin is sinned.

A Noble Fire

Education is a joy, thrill, hope
    It is a fascinating encounter
        Of the souls of students and teacher.

Education should be a sincere prayer
    Offered in the name of
        The Great Cosmic Teacher Divine.

Education can be a noble fire
    Burning out all the undesirable stuff
        In the personality of the student.

Educaton must be a rebirth
    Which takes place in the learner
        Because of the infinite hope of the teacher.

Education must be a rebirth
    Which arises in the whole class
        When amazing insights are discerned.

147

Education will be a marvelous miracle
Through which students become
Framers of a new history and a new world.

This is a Choice Too

When we do not
Have enough data
To guide us

The choice of
Not making a choice
Is a good choice

Hasty decisions
Have really ruined
The whole land

Demoralizing effects
Of the last war
Still seen everywhere

"Smoked Silver"[1]

Romance can be gay
Like the poinsettia flower
Adorning sunny California.

But the kind of romance
Which education needs
Is akin to "smoked silver"

---

1. Specially processed so as to look unassuming, without
a high polish.

It is charming and choice
  Precious and pretty too
    And yet it is nobly subdued

Here is a symbol of Zen
  Which is quiet and yet
    Speaking one million words of peace

The Kitchen Class

Usually cooking is done
  By ladies in the kitchen
    Clean and full of good food.

Occasionally courting is done
  By young people in the kitchen
    Where sweet words are exchanged.

Here at Coe this Daehler-Kitchin is used
  For the study of truth
    With all its esoteric taste and flavor

The snack of truth is akin to
  That of the Japanese *Sukiyaki*
    With beef, vegetables, and sea food.

All the delicious tastes you enjoy
  Are coherently represented
    By one pan of sukiyaki.

So this is reminding us
  Of the kaleidoscopic unity
    Of the values of civilization.

As good food pleases a hungry man
  So God makes ecstatic those who are
    Hungry and thirsty after compassion.

149

Romance should be in education;
   Poetry in the love of philosophy;
      The kitchen a part of the class-room.

The Final

If the instructor should ask
   A very difficult question
      At the final examination

Write: Education begins in after life
   If he gives a low grade
      Think: God sees your inherent worth

Confidence

The word love has been abused
   By its association with sex
      The misuse of freedom, licentiousness.

My feeling toward this group
   Is better expressed by confidence
      At its noblest and rarest.

How deep, high, broad is my confidence
   In you members of this group
      Let me count the ways.

It is infinite-dimensional and so
   Beyond all the testimony of sight
      As the rainbow is above the trees and hills.

It is not so cold as the coherence
   Of modern mathematics, advanced
      However multi-faceted it may be.

It is not so inhuman as the sea
   Of clouds below you as your
      Jet plane is near to the realm of heaven.

It is beautiful with my prayer
   Most sincere, heartfelt, ardent
      Which God will listen to and approve.

This confidence of mine will be sure
   To bring fragrant fruit of every type
      Until you usher in a new realm of happiness.

Koan[1] Today

If your teacher should ask
   A difficult question at the final
      Write: "Education is self-education"

If the teacher sees a white paper
   With no good answer written
      By the student, an "A" should be given.

Two things hopelessly far-fetched
   Should be interconnected
      In the spirit of Zen intuition.

If the Administration should
   Dismiss the unusually lenient teacher
      He should teach in another school.

All this realized by the student
   Would make him so sympathetic
      With the teacher that he'll do his best.

Applied Aesthetics

   To know beauty
      Is to see reality
         In its entirety

---

1. Device to illumine a hidden value. A Zen concept.

To aim at equality
   Is the first necessity
      For bringing amity

Let us face reality
   Which is infinity
      Enabling us to go over satiety

Hunger

I am hungry but know
   A meal is waiting for me
      Meat, vegetables, coffee

Folks are hungry in Asia
   Without knowing when
      They can be affluent

In America hunger is
   A joyous expectation
      In Asia it is fear

The Tiny Cross

To live means
   To bear a cross
      Somewhere, somehow.

It may be tiny
   And trivial
      And unnoticed.

So everyone
   Is an imitation
      Of Christ Jesus.

His cross
Is world-wide
And vicarious.

Ours is
Light and
Local too.

Let us bear
Our crosses
For others too.

The highest bliss
Is in the shadow
Of the biggest cross.

Whispers

Half an hour
With a Jewish child
Who told me his secrets.

He whispered to me
That his mommy
Did not know them.

Children usher in
The realm of heaven
Prophesied by Christ.

Howard Parsons

Seldom do I find
A philosopher who thinks
The same way I do.

153

How delighted I am
  To see in Howard
    A truly like-minded thinker.

The insights of Whitehead
  Radhakrishnan, spanning
    Old and New, East and West.

His rare appreciation
  Of a small minority cause
    Inspired me through and through.

He and I stand face to face
  Though we come from East and West
    Thus weaving unity into philosophy.

We are ordained ministers
  Though functioning in class
    Making love prevail here on earth.

Howard S. Greenlee

You graciously greeted me
  At the Cedar Rapids Airport
    Thus ushering in a new era for me.

Your Christian hospitality
  Extended to me in your home
    Has been a source of solace to me.

You kindly cooperated
  In issuing two booklets,
    Zeal for Zen, A Seven-hued Rainbow.

Helen has honored me
  With her benign presence
    In the auditorium where I teach.

154

Let us make Coe flourish
In the noblest sense of the term:
Academically excellent, socially benign.

Mental Incubation

Write here and now
Even one word or phrase
Which is a blessing indeed.

The law of mental incubation
Will be in operation
Once you begin to write.

Then all your reading,
Observation and experience
Will come to the rescue.

The nucleus of a snow-ball
Is tiny and insignificant
But attracts so much snow around it.

Now is the best moment
To get started splendidly
On this process of accumulation.

To a Ph.D. Student

I still have a nightmare
About the terror of
The long grind of the Ph.D. work.

The perspective of two decades
Gives me this wisdom
Which I would share with you.

The charm of the goal
Must not wholly minimize
The value of the process itself.

Step by step you move
Toward the goal lying ahead
With all the holiness of a halo.

The whole process of this approach
And not just the goal itself
Is a series of privileges.

Which is more meaningful,
The long process or the goal?
By all means the former.

The moment you receive the degree
You will envisage another goal
Far more attractive and worthy.

Do It Everyday

Wrestlers wrestle everyday
This is the only secret
Of their strength.

Poets too write everyday
Some heartfelt lines
Of *Haiku* ditties.

So writing becomes easy
Enjoyable and soul-consoling
As words flow, lines frame.

Write wherever you can
What you have felt
Sincerely and intensely.

156

Haiku is the language
Of the inmost core
Of every human soul.

Tea

Whiskey inebriates
Coffee stimulates
Tea merely soothes.

Haiku merely soothes
Without the strong effect
Of whiskey or coffee.

A matter of taste
I am no dictator
In this realm of choice.

My choice of tea
Is due to my appreciation
Of a soft, subdued flavor.

Good luck to you
You whiskey-drinkers
And coffee-tasters, too.

Lorine and Francis

You went the second mile
When you were kind to me
At Lisle, Boston, Pigeon Cove.

You fed and clothed my family
As we were in the midst of
The confusion of a war-torn city.

You went the fourth mile
As you found for me
A college position here.

157

You take care of Noriko
   As a member of your family
      Thus going another mile.

God will richly bless
   Your splendid ministry
      Ushering in the Kingdom of His.

Even the best biography
   Is a thin caricature
      Of personality at its best.

May my description above
   Not be too much of
      A disgrace to you two.

Lucile

This is an age of restlessness
   Which would greatly distress
      The study-loving soul of Confucius.

Even in a place of learning
   The cause of scholarship
      Is not always a supreme concern.

You have been a scholar
   Who truly loves and enjoys
      Scholarship for its own sake.

You have achieved much
   In the realm of literature
      The noble record of life itself.

Your gift and talent
   Will bring a fragrant fruit
      Unique in loveliness and lustre.

Ruth

You may not recognize
  But have helped me greatly
    By loaning me a book.

This is merely one example
  Of your kind thoughtfulness
    Which has inspired me deeply.

Your stimulating talk
  On your Berlin experience
    Will never be forgotten.

Accept my sincere prayer
  Offered in blissful gratitude
    And in heartfelt spontaneity.

Your future promises
  Are full of golden meaning
    And vermilion-tinted splendor.

Success

Ah, Golgotha with God's son
  Crimson with the westering sun
    He knew that he had won

Ere the westering sun
  Approached the golden horizon
    He knew that he had won

It should seem to none
  That a new realm he had not won
    A fruitful failure was the death of God's son

Political achievement he scored none
  Ethically and religiously he had won
    Such as to be called God's son

159

Ere the westering sun
  Reached the illumined horizon
  He knew that he had won

The Best Ways to Bliss

What sounds like impossible
  Ways of life turns out to be
  The best ways to my own bliss.

Love, Zen, Jen are these
  Impossible but important
  Ways to my own blessedness.

Love teaches utter self-sacrifice
  Bearing the cross daily
  Dying in the name of Christ.

Zen teaches boundless compassion
  Teaching to think of others first
  Myself last of all.

Jen is the ethic of the ruler
  Holding himself responsible
  For all that goes wrong.

These sound like impossible
  Ways of life but turn out to be
  The best ways to my own peace.

If these are in line with
  The will of one and the same God
  I have an added reason to respect them.

Selfishness is so tenacious
  That it takes these high ideals
  To control, in case of emergency.

Education

Who travels faster
  The peacock or the swan?
    The swan is lighter, faster.

Who advances faster
  The teacher or student?
    What is our observation?

This question answered
  Will show the key to open
    The door of good education.

The teacher must grow
  Always and indefinitely
    To make education fruitful.

I would rather be
  Like a flowing stream clear
    Than a pool muddy and stale.

Boston Zen

I am from Tokyo
  But years ago
    I was in Boston.

There I was inspired
  By the German ideal
    Of *Schenkende Tugend* (*radiant virtue*)

It is unassumingly still
  But always bespeaks
    The fullness of compassion.

The happy union
  Of quietness and compassion
    Reminds me of Zen.

Then I think about God
    Who is ever tranquil
    But infinitely compassionate.

God says to us all:
    Be still and know
    That love is the soul of the world.

Tokyo, Boston, Germany
    Makes no difference
    God loves and sustains all.

Change

Zen changes
    The rigor of math
    Into enjoyment

Contemplation
    Concentration
    Exhilaration.

All rigor
    Of life eventually
    Is tamed by Zen.

Contrition, Comprehension, Cooperation

A candid self-examination
    Yields a contrition, deep and poignant.
    God, forgive us our trespasses.

When our contrition is genuine
    We see the need of comprehension
    In our dealing with men and cultures.

Our imagination fails tragically
    Our observation is shallow and wrong.
    May God make our comprehension deep.

May we see goodness in the Samaritan
　　Who is stigmatized but has an insight
　　　　Into the hidden facets of our life.

The kaleidoscopic coherence of civilization
　　Transcends the sense of discreteness
　　　　With which a casual look is obsessed.

In God all things cohere
　　In Christ there is neither East nor West
　　　　Through Him walls of hostility break down.

May we go the second mile
　　In cooperating with classes, causes,
　　　　Cultures very different from ours.

Sin has been sinned egregiously
　　War has menaced the whole world
　　　　Its sad effects impinge on us.

Oh, God, make us all contrite
　　Colossal in our comprehension
　　　　Cooperative in a truly effective way.

The Seeds

I am satisfied
　　If there is one
　　　　Good listener here.

Most teachers
　　Expect too much
　　　　Of young students.

Some day the seeds
　　I have planted
　　　　Will grow in you.

Education means
A deep gratitude
On the lecturer's part.

Cruelty and Communism

Suppose we are asked to elaborate
On the way Jesus was captured
Humiliated and crucified.

How would we feel then?
The gospel narratives of it
Are very brief and sketchy.

How would the bereaved feel
When they were asked to elaborate
On what happened in the city of Hiroshima?

As its inhabitants were killed
By the nuclear explosion
Toward the end of the last war.

We should pu. ourselves in the position
Of another city, culture, nation.
Our imagination and conscience must be sensitized.

Communism begins to be attractive
If comprehension of this kind
Does not change our inner beings.

There is so much cruelty unintended
On the part of those good people
Whose imagination is not keen enough.

To me it is easier to talk about
Mathematics than about the massacre
Of children, ladies, animals.

164

Would Japan become Christian or Communistic?
The former will be the case only when
Cruelty goes, comprehension, contrition,
cooperation come.

Some Day

You have been
Unusually good
And patient to me.

This strange speaker
Talking about Zen
Coherence and peace.

Some day you may
See what I see
Do what I do.

Until then
May God bless
Everyone of you.

Your Cooperation

ICU is indebted to you, friends in Iowa,
For the initial organization of its facilities
Especially its chapel, the center of our activity.

It is epoch-making in four respects.
Its bilinguality producing those
Who are able to interpret two races to each other.

Second, its hope to produce public servants
Who will lead the future Japan
Using their power for the cause of God.

165

Third, its task of training future diplomats
　　Who will guide Japan in her task
　　　　Of becoming a peace-maker of the world.

Fourth, its will to produce those people
　　Who will do what is disliked by society,
　　　　Such tasks the reward of which is meagre.

Or those ladies who serve as stewardesses
　　Catering to the needs of tourists aboard planes
　　　　In the precarious situation near heaven.

All these history-making pioneers
　　Will bear their individual crosses
　　　　For the sake of the crucified Lord Jesus.

Thus your contribution to the cause of ICU
　　Will bear fruit a thousandfold
　　　　In bringing a new world of peace and hope.

Boating

　　Friendship is a ship
　　　　Put on top of a car
　　　　　　The Wolfes drove to Wellman.

　　They came to invite
　　　　Us to go boating on
　　　　　　One of the Iowa lakes.

　　International friendship
　　　　Must be a big ship
　　　　　　To take mankind to Infinite Love.

Conceit, Closed-mindedness, Cruelty

　　Who kills truth?
　　　　War of every kind does.
　　　　　　Provincialism does it too.

Neither shy squirrels
   Nor inanimate things
      But strong men do it.

They are conceited
   Closed-minded, cruel
      Impersonating God himself.

It is very unfortunate
   These small men have power
      Because there are many of them.

Let us now all emulate
   Breadth, open-mindedness
      And boundless compassion.

There is joy in this way
   Hope, peace, bliss all
      Rooted in the love of God.

Zen

The kaleidoscopic doings
   Of nature and men draw
      A coherent diagram of beauty.

It further bespeaks rhythm
   An ultimate unity of direction
      Which Zen calls boundless compassion.

It is the Dharma coherence
   Construed as the Cosmic Will,
      One Crimson Heart of Compassion.

Blooming

Let us all bloom
   Like one big blossom
      Beautiful, benign and blessed.

Human

A restless night . . . .
  Ill, painful, downcast
    I resume my work.

A late breakfast
  Gives me some strength
    Ah, the sunbeam at the table.

I look up to enjoy
  The lovely sky above
    Illumined by the sun.

Suddenly my outlook
  Takes on a new value
    A new meaning bright.

I look at myself
  More objectively, saying
    Suffering makes me human.

These gleams and glooms
  Of the human mind
    Are common to all men.

I only wish more men
  Will be patient enough
    To recover from the glooms.

Calligraphy

Here are epitomized
  The hums and hues
    Of the colorful world.

Calligraphy is akin
  To a black-and-white sketch
    Which we call *sumiye,*

Simple, subdued, strong
It depicts what is
The most impressive alone.

The thrifty-brush sketch,
The one-corner style,
Means the same thing.

Unassumingly it depicts
Unbending is its spirit
Unending its aspiration.

Not Mean Here

In spite of myself
I have been mean
Toward many people.

Disliking them much
Avoiding them so that
I may be undisturbed.

However, in dealing
With my new friends here
I would be different.

How I would like to be
At my very best,
Doing superior work.

Here the piper's song
Is responded to kindly
By genuine lovers of truth.

Let us make this
A new occasion on which
A noble life will begin.

To Joseph Fletcher

Father and daughter studied with you
As you expounded a profound view
May this year introduce a new era
Into the shining history of ICU.

Zen Rapprochement

The sky of any world-view
Will begin to shine iridescent
As it welcomes Zen into itself.

Dr. Hanson

On a crowded bus
Only once I had the joy
Of chatting with you.

That memory will live
On and on as it is
Enriched by time's beautifying effect.

My Cause

The cause I'd uphold is
Change through Christ
Who views man, ages, nations

In terms of promising possibilities
Of moral maturity
And of future fruition.

170

Zen and Math

Zen saves all men
   Including all those
      Who are not elite.

It can be explained
   So simply as to be
      Understood by idiots.

It is all compassion
   With no selfishness
      With no cruelty.

But it must sometimes
   Be verified to satisfy
      The most brilliant.

Then its Dharma laws
   Must be correlated
      With findings of math.

Democracy

Zen can bring about
   The most fruitful kind
      Of democracy we know.

It is equality so thoroughgoing
   That the West has not seen
      Such a perfect form of it.

It is boundless compassion
   Inclusive of men in society
      Throughout the past, present, future.

It is the right use of power
   Wherever it is wielded
      By whatever kind of agency.

171

It is to support a minority
    Wherever it is impinged on
        By the abuse of majority might.

It is unassumingly quiet
    Although its good fruitfulness
        Permeates the whole world.

It broadens the idea of people
    Meaning by it the coherence
        Among all values and advances.

My Pain

I have suffered
    From physical pain
        Which deepens my sympathy.

I have suffered
    From a mental pain
        Which makes me compassionate.

I am suffering
    From a vicarious pain,
        Since I study Zen.

Future Hope

A fresh spring near the sea
    Ever rises anew
        After the salt tides go over it.

My trust in your growth
    Is like this spring
        Ever rising afresh,

Even when society
    Denies your inherent worth
        And you are downcast.

Squirrels

Snow has come
　Most squirrels
　　Have disappeared.

This morning snowy
　One squirrel
　　Is near my window.

I pray sincerely
　That all squirrels
　　Have enough to eat.

Fruitful

Moralists are preachy
　Philosophers irritable
　　But Zen is benign.

Zen is a smile
　That has no cynicism
　　But is all mercy.

It is calm, peace
　But has helpful hints
　　Ideas that work.

Hidden Zen

Zen at its best
　Is not in the temple
　　In some dark nook of the world.

Zen worthy of the name
　Is found in all men
　　All things in the process of growth.

We see a hidden Zen
    In art, science, peace
        All flowers of culture.

Photos of Hiroshima

Action is not always good,
    Efficiency is spelt cruelty:
        So say these photos from Hiroshima.

Power is not always good,
    Its abuse kills innocent folk
        In the most brutal massacre.

Ethic is not for the weak alone
    The weak are more or less
        Humble, meek, cooperative.

Who soiled the history of men
    Drenching it in the boiling blood
        Of those who died in agony?

Who caused the recent centuries
    To be sick with retaliation?
        The strong have done that.

The world can get along well
    With the weak, mediocre, tired,
        But it must teach ethic to the strong.

Do not say ethic is idealistic
    It is really needed by the strong
        In this powerful age of ours.

174

Chinese Poems

Here the pattern is four-dimensional
Like a four-petaled iris
Adorning the inner garden
Of the Meiji Shrine in Tokyo.

The first line introduces
A vivid impression of life
Deeply felt and dearly cherished
In the inner shrines of the heart.

The second line elaborates
On the meaning of the idea
Already happily introduced
By the beginning of the poem.

The third is attention-compelling
In going beyond the order
Which the first two lines
Have depicted with felicity.

Beauty is a pattern whose beauty
Is saved from becoming a boredom
Only through transcendence
Of the first pattern framed.

Thus a new dimension of growth
Is added to the loveliness
Of the poem whose conclusion
Is adorned with the last line.

To Eleanore Ramsey

Your noble attentiveness in class
Our talks in your social room
All this is a sweet memory to me.

You often looked sad and serious
That worried me for I felt
That something was troubling you.

But your papers when they came
Made me delighted to understand
How much you have learned from me.

8 December
(Dogen, *True Dharma Nuclear Treasury,* vol. 16)

On the eighth of December, 428 B.C.
Buddha was squatted at the foot
Of the Bodhi tree in Magadha.

As dawn was breaking that morn
He saw the togetherness of all things
Of the past, present, and future.

The Pearl Harbor Attack was
Conducted on the morning of
The eighth of December, 1941.

Every war ever fought in history
Was fought in the name of religion.
Here is what makes us deeply pensive.

A casual acquaintance shows differences:
A profound insight sad similarities
Among ethics, religions, philosophies.

The tradition should be related to
The best insight of civilization
So that coherence may guide us.

The colossal coherence of history
Bespeaks the presence of God
Whose will is unity, peace, humility.

Professor Lindsay

A kind, effective teacher
A handsome gentleman
Teaching advanced calculus.

He is really inspiring
So that many students come
And follow his guidance.

He is very genuine and
Humble enough to apologize
In class and outside of the class.

Functioning in a college
He ushers in hopefulness,
Courage to resume hard tasks.

May God bless richly
This promising scholar
Who is adorned with a halo.

East and West

Through the grace of God
I have looked at the West
Science, philosophy, history.

But though I enjoy all this
I still miss the fragrance of the East
Which is the flower of compassion.

Quietly and unassumingly Zen marches on
Amidst the noise and haste of this day
Doing the work of truth-seeking.

Peace and compassion and grace
Beckon to me as I walk on this road
While approaching the western values too.

East and West, Old and New
   With all their unique treasures
      Adorn this way of vast coherence.

The most impressive togetherness which I see
   Is the red, white, blue togetherness,
      Mental, material, and mathematical.

The mind is red with zeal and love
   The material is white with calm and energy
      The mathematical is blue with depth and mystery.

The colossal coherence of the cosmos
   Is thus shining with three hues
      Passionately red, calmly white, deeply blue.

Connection

   Philosophy and poetry
      Education and romance
         Are interrelated.

   These four types
      Of human experiences
         Should be always together.

   Poetry and romance disclose
      The charm of a noble realm
         Which is half-concealed, half-revealed.

   Like a Zen man Whitehead
      Shows the interconnectedness
         Of these four enterprises.

   Philosophy and education
      Would die without the halo
         Of poetry and romance.

178

The Dharma (Law)

If anything good was said in class
  It is solely due to the Dharma
    Which sustains all things everywhere.

If you have done anything good
  That is your devotion to the Dharma
    Though you may not see that rootage.

I am merely a spokesman of the Dharma
  So that no credit is due me at all
    And all the blunder is due to me.

The kaleidoscopic doings of men and nature
  Wherever they are good, lovely, true
    Are due to the compassion of the Dharma.

Art, music, poetry, education,
  Science, religion, philosophy, mathematics
    Are all so many hues and hums of the Dharma.

So seeing, I am grateful and humble
  Praising my friends, blaming no one
    Loving, enduring, hoping all things.

The voice of Zen is fourfold:
  The multitudes are infinitely many
    So they all must be enlightened.

The lower desires are infinitely tenacious
  But they must all be transmuted
    Into so many facets of compassion.

The Dharma truth is infinitely rich
  All of it must be studied and mastered
    So that truth-seeking may be complete.

179

The Dharma deed is infinitely many-faceted
But it must be realized completely
So that the realm of peace may come.

The Test of Truth

Clarity has four facets
And their coherence
Serves as the test of truth.

Clarity due to perception
Is not so convincing
As common sense thinks.

Aristotle, Hume, Ayer
Relied on this clarity
Against the Zen contention.

When Buddha practiced Zen
His eyes were open
Respecting perception and intuition.

When Descartes meditated
His eyes were closed
He trusted only mathematical intuition.

Clarity due to correspondence
Is what mathematics uses
Guiding sophisticated men.

Clarity becomes more comprehensive
Through coherence
Among all values and facts.

Thus civilization itself
Would guide us convincingly
Through its kaleidoscopic vista.

180

This kaleidoscopic coherence
 Would best sustain
  Tradition at its most profound.

Synoptic self-evidence will be
 The most reason-satisfying test
  Of the most comprehensive truth.

One meaning of civilization
 Is the illumination of mystery
  In the vague, cosmic background.

Sex and Zen

Let us listen to Zen
 As to how it copes with
  Temptations of all kinds:

Sex, power, laziness
 Vindictiveness and anger
  Belligerence, pride and self-pity.

Zen smiles sympathetically
 And would admit frankly
  That temptation is hard to resist.

After that Zen shows us
 That there is another way:
  That of noble self-transcendence.

The delight of realizing
 That the higher way is
  The more gratifying way.

Self-forgetfulness in truth-seeking,
 Helping those in agony,
  Is the way to self-transcendence.

After having revealed this
  Zen would reassure us all
    That we too are able to do it.

Zen adds another remark to it
  By saying that if we are tired
    We should take a good rest.

Draw a Diagram

How refreshing to draw
  A diagram or two
    After having studied for hours.

Something somewhat new
  We need to do or think
    From time to time.

From staleness and boredom
  To encouragement and ecstasy
    Through the adventure of the mind.

God encourages creativity
  Dynamic, original, epoch-making
    The dream of youth, with joy harvested.

The thrilling adventure
  Of the history-remaking spirit
    Is what God does within us.

The Last and Best Zen

Each time Dogen squatted
  He prayed that his Zen
    May be the best he ever practiced.

As if he were to have
  The very last Zen practice
    In all his life and career.

This class of mine should be
So conducted that I may not
Regret even if I die this month.

Let us welcome each moment
As if it were the final end
Of the history of mankind.

The present moment alone
Is the divinest moment
When God works wonders.

Ah, the scintillating splendor
And the illumining insight
Of this present moment marvelous.

Whitehead

Believing in the hidden genius
Of every student of his
Whitehead taught for half a century.

All students of his class
Became "A" students excellent
Because of his constant encouragement.

Thus his boundless hope
Transformed all men and women
Who came under his magnetic charm.

We members of this Coe class
Study his character so that
We too may all be "A" students.

Education begins in after life
Like a cloud shining iridescent
With the brilliance of the setting sun.

So let us continue to hope
  Even beyond any evidence
    Under the all-loving God of grace.

Long patience yields genius
  Nurtured by the happy union
    Of drill and dream, reading and resilience.

The Fragrant Past

Occasionally the past
  Takes on a value
    Faint but fragrant.

It is as fragrant
  As a sweet cake
    Fresh from the oven.

Then at present
  We take courage
    The future brightens.

One-to-many
  Correspondence
    Saves the day.

Zen is akin
  To a symphony
    Of inspiration.

Life is hard
  But this hardship
    Itself is the Dharma.

184

God in Gall

To him who has been ill
  Health is a great bliss
    Filling him with ecstasy.

To him who has sinned
  Good is a bright flash
    Filling him with enchantment.

To him who has been alone
  Friends are a noble thrill,
    Filling him with gratitude.

God works in sickness
  Sinfulness and solitariness.
    He loves all in agony.

One with Hope

When our task is hard
  God, give us the titan's might
    The martyr's will unbending.

Resolve, resilience, reserve
  Longsuffering divine;
    Oh, God sustain us.

We are to build a new realm
  Where love and reason prevail
    Peace and equality reign.

Teach us how to pray
  So that we may be refilled
    With the superabundance of grace.

Reorient, recreate, reinforce
  Our inner beings sublime
    Till we are one with hope itself.

Sawai

Professor Sawai
  Sat to my left
    In the farewell party.

He to Oxford
  I to America
    We flew.

Before he reached
  Oxford University . . .
    A heart-attack.

The same death
  Buddha once thought of
    Has taken him.

May he and
  Members of his
    Family have God's grace.

Being born but
  Dying eventually
    We live in Zen truth.

Miss A

Miss A's face
  Brightened with joy
    To hear me say,

"You have written
  An A paper
    Which is excellent."

How I wish
  Coe would allow me
    To give all A's.

Non-discrimination
  Is the truth
    Of ultimate reality.

The togetherness
  Of the whole class
    Is important.

The togetherness
  Of all the world
    Is what counts.

Efficient and Benign

Efficiency is sometimes spelt
  Cruelty, cut-throat competition.
    Here is a value mixed with a disvalue.

But Zen urges to sacrifice
  Efficiency for the sake of mercy:
    All others first and generate peace.

Christ too shows two criteria:
  One higher and the other lower
    The higher for me, the lower for others.

He who is not with me is against me
  He who is not against me is for me.
    Thus Christ prefers love to efficiency.

When efficiency is united with love
  Which sacrifices its will to power
    The peace of God will be here.

Dogen's Zen

I am merely a fire-fly
  Giving a dim light faint
    To one dark nook of this vale.

187

But the Buddha is like
  The full moon near the Zenith
  Illumining the whole sky above.

As I practice Zen in my hut
  The dawn stars are burning away
  Prophesying the coming of the crimson morn.

The pagoda-like cloud formation
  Soars high up into the zenith
  As chrysanthemum fragrance fills the air.

I do not need the purple gown
  Given me by the gracious Emperor
  Only this black one is enough for me.

My whole being is dedicated
  To the education of young Buddhists
  Who will fulfill the Dharma cause.

Maple leaves in the autumnal season
  Snow and hail in winter
  The young foliage in spring

The cicada music in summer
  In this mountain temple of mine,
  All this is one voice of compassion.

Our Task

  Pacify and pray
    Pray and pacify
    Wholeheartedly and always

  For that is indeed
    The will of God
    In Christ resurrected

188

Beautify and bless
  Bless and beautify
    Abundantly and always

For that is indeed
  The will of God
    In Christ exalted

Marvel and march
  March and marvel
    Ecstatically and ever

Our eternal pilgrimage
  Under the banner of God
    Is adorned with wondrous gems.

Faith and Reason

Once upon a time
  War was waged
    Between faith and reason.

This civil war
  Has caused sad effects
    In the life of men today.

Let us reframe now
  Faith as a function
    Or correspondence between values.

Reason should mean
  Correspondence among
    All values and facts.

Through this correspondence
  Faith will be benign
    Toward all correspondences.

189

Music

"Around an open fire we get all warm
  Just like Zen should inspire"
"In tense moments when we feel low,
  We should think of Zen and feel an inner glow."
"If Christmas was in May, we could
  Still help others and make them feel gay."
"To keep from being tired to Zen class
  I go, to be inspired."
"Frustrations can be quelled by love,
  Just like anger can be calmed by Zen."
"What a refreshing thing music is,
  It brings to me a pure plan."

Judy Christiansen

In Response to Judy's Haiku

Music is enchanting
  Thrilling us through and through
    Here Zen is what gives life to it.

Zen opens our spiritual ear
  Making audible everywhere
    The symphony of heavenly rhythm.

Space and Time make music
  As Zen attunes our ear
    To the harmony of the cosmos.

Stars and the cloud sing
  Melodiously and majestically
    As Zen comes into our beings.

The temple bell rings at midnight
  One hundred and eight times
    To remind us of boundless compassion.

Even when the bell is still
It continues to make music
Filling us with cosmic peace.

The flower-decorated sutra
Discloses the civilized history
Full of the music of quiet loveliness.

'From Student to Teacher. . . .'

Enriched!
As one who finds
One red rich rose
. . . in a Winter Lane.

Susan Engelhardt

Prayerfully

The end of the term draws near
I feel already nostalgic
For members of this class.

Your cooperation, attention
Patience has been appreciated.
I shall long remember this class.

It is great to meet friends
But sad to have to part from them.
I would entrust you all to God.

So farewell to you. May you be
Well, happy, blessed in every way.
May we meet again at least once more.

An instructor pours his whole soul
Into the hearts of his students
That they may be truly successful.

191

Your future is bright, promising
Under the care of the mighty God
Who is the Lord of history and the world.

God as Order

At the dawn of history
When men admire tyrants
Gods are like whimsical persons.

Touchy, vain, imperious
Kings, who are jealous, impatient,
Predetermined to punish noble men.

Love and Zen learn from history
Thus attributing to Ultimate Reality
Benignity, patience, order, peace.

That ultimate unity of direction
In the universe, lovely, mysterious,
Axiogenesis and axiosoteria.

Impartiality, creativity, adventure
Generating and sustaining all law
In the mental, material, mathematical realms.

God cares for us all men
With the cumulative convincingness
Of the kaleidoscopic coherence cosmic.

Parental Prayer

Parents everywhere
Regardless of their creeds
Pray most ardently.

Their prayer for
　　Dear children of theirs
　　　Is altruism itself.

A complete and
　　Thoroughgoing self-forgetfulness
　　　In that parental prayer.

Buddha's love is
　　The generalization
　　　Of such a prayer.

He was a father too
　　Of Rahula, "Obstacle"
　　　His only son.

The Parable of Persimmons

Puckery persimmons
　　Become the sweetest
　　　Fruit in the world.

Not sinfulness exactly
　　But smallness is
　　　What Zen warns against.

Optimistic in some
　　Thoroughgoing way
　　　Is the faith of Zen.

This method
　　May not always work
　　　But no method does.

It has changed
　　Puckery persons
　　　Into sweet souls.

193

It is rooted in
   Comprehensive coherence
   Cosmic Compassion.

Death and Dharma (Law)

Sooner or later
   Death calls on
   All human beings.

There is something
   Totally inevitable
   About its coming.

It will destroy
   Not only the lives of men
   But their selfish creed.

The creed of power,
   Plausible to common sense,
   Thus shows its weakness.

But mercy boundless
   Lives on and on
   Throughout all history.

So realizing
   Buddha's selfish fear
   Dies like a mist.

This is the fruit
   Of his Zen experience
   At the Bodhi tree.

He said, "I may die
   But my loved ones
   Endure and flourish."

To be selfish
   Means to have
      No one whom to love.

Altruism offers
   All mankind
      And posterity to love.

Suddenly the future
   Begins to brighten
      With hope and bliss.

The soul is expanded
   Infinitely to include
      All men and things.

This expansion,
   Ennoblement, ecstasy
      Is the theme of Zen.

As long as one is
   Obsessed with himself . . .
      Gloom, fear, sorrow.

Zen ushers in
   A new cosmos
      Shining with mercy.

The thought of death
   Has thus disclosed
      The law of compassion.

Political Predicaments

Sandwiched between
   The two strongest nations:
      Kosala and Magadha.

The small Sakya realm
Was precarious indeed.
This Buddha realized.

He somehow felt
That Kosala might someday
Ruin his father's castle.

So his fear of death
Has not only individual
But also tribal roots.

During Buddha's lifetime
Kosala did annihilate
The people of this castle.

In 1967 Buddha
Fears lest nuclear war
Should ruin the world.

Boundless compassion
Has an added meaning
In this age of ours.

Still Hated

Christians love all enemies
But one enemy they still see
In the rigorous study of math.

Jesus came to bear witness
To the truth of life, man, the world.
Truth-seeking is aided by math.

Today he would urge us
To love our study of math:
Zero, infinity, limit, integration.

Love and Zen come together
In their interest in these matters:
Zero, infinity, limit, integration.

I as a teacher of ethics
Owe you many apologies
For my constant talk of math.

But now you must have seen
Why I have done this
In the name of Zen and Love too.

You will regain self-confidence
By looking at zero, the void
How unassumingly it does its work.

Soon East and West will exchange places
The West remaining devoted to a personal God
The East will see in math laws of His will.

Dying Together

"Mother," said a girl,
"Let us die embracing
When war comes."

"Let us be together
Even through the flame
Of nuclear explosion."

In Church

Thanksgiving Day, sunshiny, brisk
A lovely service is held in church
As a token of gratitude to God.

But how many people are unable
To attend such a Christian meeting
Because of subtle reasons unexpressed.

197

There are prayers unheard
   In the hearts of frustrated folk
      Who are too dismayed to pray.

May God forgive us all
   Even those who are not articulate
      Unheard prayers are acceptable too.

Unite us all sinners everywhere
   Who have not found God as yet
      Who have rebelled against his truth.

Teach us how to transcend
   Superficial differences and barriers
      Tragic, harmful discriminations.

There are too many enemies to be loved
   Those who do not see what we see
      Identify us with our staunch enemies.

Our Chapel

Coe has a cozy chapel
   So beautiful as to make
      Even Martin Luther envious.

There at noon we meet
   Having a prayer meeting,
      Delightful and heart-warming.

Bruce, Bob, Geoff, Flo,
   Elaine, Linnea and I meet
      Thus in that cozy place at noon.

As candles are lighted
   We begin to pray to God:
      One by one in each tongue.

For those who are ill, downcast
   And have any kind of trouble
      We offer sincere prayers.

For the realization of peace
  And the fulfilment of our dreams
    We pray in the name of the Lord.

Coe has a cozy chapel
  Not attended by too many folk,
    But blessed by heavenly glow.

Forbes

Forbes knows how
  I am inspired, intoxicated
    Resurrected through God's grace.

Senior Vice President
  Of Merchants National Bank
    Is a prime pal of mine.

He and I talked
  About important matters
    On a dark street at night.

We are free thinkers
  Belonging to the same church
    Attending meetings together.

What a fresh stimulation
  Forbes has given me
    I praise God for this.

May He bless your work
  Your family most richly
    In all the years to come.

Beauty

Attempt to appreciate
  All people and situations
    As abundantly as possible

199

Beauty contemplated, created
Is the most spontaneous
And genuine kind of appreciation

My past experience
Deepened my appreciation
Of all men and situations

My introspective nature
Inhibitions, frustrations, fears
Make me appreciate people

The war years, bereavement
Inflation, starvation, insanity
Serve me as purifying incense

My revisit to America
Makes me see first-hand
The kind hospitality of friends

The seven-hued thought
Of contemporary Japan
Shines with sevenfold appreciation

So there are many causes
For my appreciation abundant
Ultimately due to the grace of God

"Blow high, blow low
Not all its snow
Could quench
The hearth-fire's ruddy glow"

This is my ideal of education
This class should be joyous
Despite all the noise of the world

Apathy is everywhere
Appreciation is rare
This class-room is rare

In this sheltered context
    We nurture our appreciation
        To be extended out into the world

Marx said, "Change it"
    We say, "Understand first
        Appreciate the hidden treasures"

Spinoza freely interpreted:
    Ethics is convincing only when
        Math is incorporated into it

India says: Include
    China begs: Change
        I plead: Appreciate

Appreciation means freedom
    From impatience, anger, scathing words
        Retaliation, apathy, enmity

Humiliated I think of Christ
    Fatigued I think of Buddha
        Hopeless I think of Confucius

In this valley of tears
    Let us be gladness-breeders
        Engendering compassion and love

Beauty means among other things
    Interaction with the milieu
        Extending itself to larger contexts

Haste, hatred, haughtiness
    Are what appreciation
        Would go over patiently

Love is a red rose
    Jen is a blue iris
        Zen a purple violet

Parables

For four thousand years
   Until 1882 when Lindemann
     Solved the problem of squaring the circle

The human mind relied on
   The naive method of ruler and compasses
     Using sense-perception as a guide

Lindemann solved the enigma
   By higher analysis of algebra
     Using infinite expansion of i, e, log

Here Jesus would speak a parable:
   Sense shows only discrete surfaces
     Beneath which lies interconnectedness

Euler's theorem
   Correlates arithmetic, algebra, trig
     The mutual dependence of i, π and e

For four thousand years
   Ethics and religions relied on
     The testimony of sense perception

Right and wrong, above and below,
   Friend and foe, believer and heretic
     Are too naively differentiated

This way men can not solve
   The recurring problem of war
     Until the faith of Jesus intervenes

The sun shines upon just and unjust
   Sending the gracious rain on
     All men, inanimate things, atoms

202

Samaritans have virtues rare
    Which the world should respect
        Thus breaking down walls of hostility

Mankind is one vast unity
    Under One Father who works
        Through, above, in everything

The so-called heathens are
    Our invaluable helpers
        Who can enrich our own views

Boston Revisited

Twenty-three years afterwards
    Boston without Doctor Brightman
        But Bertocci, Lavely flourish

Mt. Vernon and Joy Streets
    Beacon Press, Carl Seaburg
        Hopes and recollections swirl

Tom and I in Boston
    Feeling cold fingers of the rain
        Soaked but strangely moved

At two o'clock before dawn
    In the Statler-Hilton Hotel
        Followers of Christ and Marx met

Crab-meat, caviar, cheese
    A frank talk on tensions
        Ways to peace and truth

Boston has remained the same
    But Tokyo was utterly ruined
        And has been resurrected anew

Ah, Boston where Brightman taught
 Today Mrs. Brightman, Bertocci
  Lavely, Millard are benign

Thanks to two Howards
 I have revisited Boston
  The star of my aspiration

Three Marxist thinkers
 Absolutize Karl's writing
  Seeing nothing noble elsewhere

Karl Marx absolutized
 A sad contrast to the Vedas
  Enriched, remoulded as time goes on

Most scholars resemble
 Archaeological museums mouldy
  No spark of creative venture

Jesus beckons to us from above
 To seek and knock so that
  We may be as perfect as God

To follow him means for us
 To bear witness to the truth
  Going beyond stale stereotypes

Dawn Hike

After two o'clock at dawn
 Parsons and I hiked
  Back to the Y.M.C.A. Hotel

We had just attended
 An informal gathering
  Held in the room of Soviet friends

How unforgettable all this
  Unusual get-together
    And the dawn hike of ours

The gathering was held
  In the Statler-Hilton Hotel
    An old triangular building

John Somerville also
  Was in that gathering
    Held after the regular meeting

America, Russia, Japan
  Met and talked intimately
    In the name of philosophy

During that hike of ours
  I was exhilarated
    Because of Parsons' kindness

Death, destruction, stared at,
  Make us intensely appreciative
    If we survive the crisis

"Inspirations we have shared together. . . .
  Their Fruit is the Prayer they bring."

                  Antoinette Kirchner

An Iowa Lake

A frozen lake, dead grass
  Oak trees, bare and brown
    The sunset tawny and tainted

The cemetery half-buried with snow
  Flowers mark family affections
    The sunset bespeaks a benediction

205

In a Chicago restaurant gay
  The head-waiter gave me a menu
    Saying: "Don't throw it away, come again"

From Chicago to Cedar Rapids
  Tom drove the college station-wagon
    I jotted down Haiku on the menu

Back in Cedar Rapids, Iowa
  Where wonderful friends wait for me
    How blessed to resume teaching here

The Farm Market near my house
  Shopping is a joy, the like of which
    I had never enjoyed in Tokyo

The second of January greets me
  As kindly as friends on streets
    Where I am saluted with a cheer

They come to me on the street
  Greeting me, shaking my hand
    As if they were relatives of mine

The spirit of Christ flourishes
  Here on the icy street of Iowa
    I wish Tokyo could be like this

Regular Coffee

In a Boston Cafeteria
  The waitress spoke of
    Regular coffee

I did not at first
  Understand the meaning
    Of what she said

206

Regular coffee has
   Cream and sugar in it
      Man has love and hope

A heavenly being
   Visiting the world today
      Shocked to meet loveless men

Regular men must have
   Love and hope always
      Regardless of race and creed

Loveless men with no hope
   Are not regular but rare
      In the sight of heavenly beings

Fatigued

Fatigued, frustrated, fearful
   I lie down to take a rest
      Even before the coming of night

Comparatively privileged I am
   Being a college professor
      With friends good, trustworthy

How many folk in the world
   Fatigued, frustrated, fearful
      Without friends and employment

New Year

A great ecstasy arises
   In the soul of the Japanese
      As New Year comes

It is ushered in
   By the temple bell
      Ringing 108 times

This great number means
   Tenaciousness of selfishness
      To be transmuted into mercy

Thus transmuted the self
   Becomes a new servant
      Of radiant, boundless mercy

The mercy-radiating self
   Is the enlightened one
      With nothing but service infinite

New Year clothes sky and sea
   With a purple hue heavenly
      Consistent, boundless compassion

Time is so merciful as to
   Make New Year an occasion
      On which we can all be new

We do not grow older but newer
   Through the all-renewing magic
      Of Eternal Time, All Compassion

Jesus at the age of twelve
   Listened to the Jewish tradition
      Asking it startling questions

Plato quit writing poems
   As he became a philosopher
      But philosophy is akin to poetry

Sometimes the right choice for us
   Is the choice of both values
      Which seem to conflict on the surface

The casual eye sees contradictions
   But a profound insight discerns
      A comprehensive coherence in life

Jesus came to break down
All walls of hostility
In and outside of men and nations

Christ urges us to create
New values, vivid hopes
To remake history and the world

Forgetting what lies behind us
We are to strive forward
Toward the shining City of God

Christ is the brightest symbol
Of the realm of hope to be
Ushered in the history of men

We Christian theologians
Should not follow Marxists
Absolutizing their symbol of truth

New dreams, myriad-tinted
Must guide us on to the vision
Of the future fulfilment of God's will

Learning from astro-physics
Social science and mathematics
The mind must prove its uniqueness

This uniqueness will be shown
In its vision of eternal God
The source of love and loveliness

Mental, material, mathematical
The world is three-dimensional
Under the triune God of Christ

Buddha "zenned", Aristotle walked
Descartes meditated, Gandhi fasted
Today the computer does our work

Pammy Sue Brenneman

You will be six
   On the sixth day
      Of the sixth month, 1966

Six is a good number
   Meaning a long life
      According to Japanese tradition

You will usher in
   The Kingdom of Peace
      Lasting forever

Pammy, you have a mission
   Giving a long life
      To the world of men

Satori

What used to be trying
   Has become thrilling, joyous;
      Due to inner change of mind itself

What used to be boring
   Has become blessed, ecstatic
      Due to rebirth of self itself

What used to be impossible
   Has become inspiring, fascinating
      Due to disclosure of Dharma itself

Thus is born a new creature
   Able to cope with all things
      Changing them into beatitudes

Now the sky is goldenly gilded
   The earth takes on a divine color
      The soul is filled with enlightenment

Compassion

The sun shines, the sky is blue,
Always above the cloud, mist, haze
Compassion is thoroughgoing, never failing

Already in January here in Iowa
The atmosphere is springy, gay
As if to declare that God is near

In this wide world wonderful
One thing counts, one alone,
Love sacrificial which God bestows

Love is the front gate to God;
Zen the back gate unknown;
Jen the subway submerged

You are academic people
Hence my deep exposition of Zen
To common folk it is compassion

A big stone will never float
However hard you may pray
So all laws obey compassion

Compassion brings the greatest fruit
Only if we believe in it
Under all circumstances imaginable

He who says it does not work
Is he who has never tried it
Stake your whole being on it alone

God

He works through America
  Teachers like Brightman, Bennett, Brooks
    Friends and students I deal with

He works through America
  Her sight, sound and scent
    The sky, stars, sea, shining

Teaching us all three things:
  Contrition, comprehension, cooperation
    Which bring about appreciation abundant.

Christ came to inculcate
  Contrition, comprehension, cooperation
    To usher in the Kingdom of Peace

In this nuclear age of ours
  West and East must unite
    Through mutual appreciation abundant

Suicide

In 1935 a Japanese physicist
  Predicted the π meson, namely,
    A new elementary particle

Militant Japan began a war
  In 1941 and has been
    Completely destroyed

It is a suicide on the part
  Of an intellectual
    But Godless nation

Beware of mesons
  Which must be put
    To moral uses God approves

212